Words Not Spoken

Understanding the Pastor's Silent Hurts

by

Stewart Simms

To my lovely friend and sister in Christ
Lou Robinson

I love you and rejoice in serving Christ with you.

Stewart Simms
Aug 7, 2011

ISBN: 978-0-88144-167-3

Foreword

My friend, Stewart Simms, has written a book that has long been needed. Stewart is uniquely qualified to write such a book about understanding the pastor's silent hurts because of his extensive pastoral ministry, much of it under one church. It can be much more challenging to have an effective ministry at a single location than it is to move often in one's ministry. A long tenure means that you must live transparently and deal openly with your own humanity and that of the members of your church. Further, Stewart is a student of the Word and that will come through as you read this book that often reads like a stimulating Bible study.

But don't let the title fool you! This is not simply a book that will help you to better understand and support your minister; it is so much more than that. Stewart writes honestly about matters such as loneliness, resentment, comparison, prayerlessness, sadness, disappointment, and family failures—matters that confront all of us. This book will help you understand yourself and others. But it goes beyond helping you understand these human dilemmas; it sets you on a path for healing. It is not only descriptive, it is also prescriptive.

Since I am both the son of a pastor and a pastor myself, I want to commend this book to every congregation. It should be required reading. Pastoral turnover and pastoral burnout have been well-documented by researchers, too many to mention. There can be little question that ministry is unique in its demands and in its risks. Stewart has written passionately and compassionately about these matters. He has revealed a sense of openness in a tasteful manner that will allow you to look into the life and pains of your minister without feeling like you are prying or eaves-dropping. Stewart doesn't whine about the challenges of life and ministry, he openly and honestly shares from his heart in the hope that this book will help build up the church as we learn to minister to one another.

I enjoy the way Stewart moves from personal illustration to biblical example and then biblical prescription. You will discover that this book provides insightful Bible study that is both enjoyable and challenging. I have long maintained that "nothing changes anyone's life but the Word of God applied by the Spirit of God." This book follows that simple axiom. Stewart doesn't simply describe the "silent hurts"; he helps us know how to give and accept healing based on solid biblical principles.

As a pastor and as one who has had the responsibility of training young pastors, I want you to read this book and then pass it along to others. Better yet, study it together with a small group of believers. You will be blessed, your pastor will be encouraged, your church will be strengthened, and the kingdom will be advanced.

Ken Hemphill, National Strategist for Empowering Kingdom Growth (SBC)

Contents

Acknowledgement

During the summer between my junior and senior years of high school, I was encouraged by my parents to go to summer school to take a course in typing, taught by Mrs. Charles Smith. I was told that I would always benefit from having that skill. I took the course, but I have always been a slow typist. For years, I resisted getting a computer with word processing capabilities for my office. Though I finally relented due to pressure from my staff, and though I now enjoy many aspects of computer use, when it came to writing this book, how did I do it? The old fashioned way, in long hand on my yellow legal pads! I thus depended on many people with typing and computer skills far beyond my own.

So I offer thanks to secretaries, Carolyn Beam and Meg Doster, and friend, Georganne Murdock, for their proficiency at deciphering my scrawl and churning out pages. I am grateful to friends like Jim Burkett, Brad Stephenson, Stephen Edwards, Richard Gray and others, and to my wife, Dianne, for their patient reading of my manuscript, practical suggestions, and encouragement to proceed. My brother, Robert, and my mother, Mary Ann, have also been great encouragements along the way. Seminary professors Dr. Budd Smith and Dr. Al Fasol invited me to present selections from these chapters in their classes at Southwestern Baptist Theological Seminary and then encouraged me to follow through. Rev. and Mrs. Marshall Collins (Sarah Lynn) offered the use of their beautiful mountain home in the hills above Mars Hill, North Carolina, for a week to finally finish the manuscript. It was that quiet week that made me decide to proceed.

Most of all, I thank Mr. Todd Rutherford, Nikki Ferguson and the staff at Yorkshire Publishing for their editing skills and advice, and for assisting me in making this first book a reality. All Scripture quotations are from the King James Version of the Bible.

Dedication

To my brother, Robert, who faced adversity during his years in ministry, beyond what I ever could imagine, and yet, persisted in following his calling. I admire him as a servant of God and value him as a preacher and writer more than he will ever know. He inspired and encouraged me to finally put these thoughts down on paper

Introduction

For many years, I have wanted to write a book that would help ministers and their congregations better understand some things about each other. That understanding is essential to a true and honest love relationship. The world of the minister is often a world of distinct contrasts. On the one hand, the minister lives in a "glass house". At times, he may feel that everyone knows everything about him and his life. People seem to know he has problems before he does. (I use the male personal pronoun for the sake of simplicity. Women in ministry positions probably are scrutinized just as carefully.) Ministers' lives often seem like front page news.

It's not just in small towns where gossip is rumored (often unfairly) to be the number one pastime. It happens in mega churches located in mega cities. Why is that? Why do people seem to pay such close attention to the minister's every move?

Maybe it is because he is generally held in fairly high esteem, and expected to be an example of purity, wisdom, discipline, and good judgment. Paul the Apostle knew that reality. So, instead of waiting for the prying eyes and the invasive questions, he willingly made his life an open book. He invited close inspection. For example, when he bid a tearful goodbye to leaders of the church at Ephesus, he said,

> Ye know, from the first day that I came into Asia, after what manner I have been with you at all seasons, serving the Lord with all humility of mind and with many tears, and

temptations which befell me by the lying in wait of the Jews: And that I kept back nothing that was profitable unto you, but have shewed you, and have taught you publickly, and from house to house, testifying both to the Jews and to the Greeks, repentance toward God, and faith toward our Lord Jesus Christ." (Acts 20:18b-21)

Or again, to the Christians of Thessalonica, in dealing with people being unwilling to work for their living, Paul wrote,

For yourselves know how ye ought to follow us: for we behaved not ourselves disorderly among you: Neither did we eat any man's bread for nought; but wrought with labour and travail night and day, that we might not be chargeable to any of you: not because we have not power, but to make ourselves an ensample unto you to follow us."
(2 Thessalonians 3:7-9)

It is clear that Paul not only knew he would be watched, he welcomed it.

There are times some pastors talk freely about their hurts and frustrations and about how hard they work, not because of any desire to be transparent and to demonstrate the sufficiency of God's grace and power, but to elicit sympathy from the people of the church. That would be an unhealthy motive for wanting to talk about how they feel. There are other times pastors don't like to admit their hurts because they feel (wrongly) they have a reputation of perfection and power to protect, and that their credibility and possibility for future success depend upon that reputation. The reputation many want to keep before the people is "super pastor," the one able to "leap tall problems with a single bound," and produce miracles on demand. To admit any hurt they feel might compromise their ability or at least their image as a leader, or prevent them from being seen as ones who are following God's plans and are being filled with God's power.

The opposite is usually true. The image they present may well be that of a fake, someone who is covering his true humanness. At the least, it does not allow people into their lives so the people will grow to know and love their pastor, and it denies the people what may be God's way of returning to their pastor the ministry they have received. Pastors often lead best from the position of being what Henri Nouwen insightfully called "a wounded healer."

Maybe it is good, in a way, for a minister to know that people do watch his life. As much as it may seem to rob him of his privacy, it might be an encouragement to keep every aspect of his life chaste and above reproach. Every minister should be able to say, even if tongue-in-cheek, "Hire someone to follow me, if you want. You won't find anything to discredit me." His public pronouncements and his private behavior should match. As intrusive as that seems, many ministries would have been saved by awareness that people do expect the best from the minister, and they are watching.

On the other hand, being on constant public view and living under high expectations can greatly complicate the minister's life when, as a very real human being, he needs help. While much of his life is inevitably in public view, there are often other things about his life he would dare not tell. There are things about his private, inner world he feels reluctant to ever reveal to anyone.

A young evangelist told of a mission trip he led to Europe. While there, he borrowed an old car from some friends. One particularly cold morning, he went to the car to drive to the mission site for the day and found that both front and rear windshields were covered with ice. According to him, there was ice not only on the outside but also on the inside of the window.

He worked for a few minutes chipping the ice away but he could remove only enough on the front through which to have a porthole view. Still, he thought it was enough to drive.

He picked up several team members and drove to the site. When they got out of the car, one young man slammed the front door closed. There was the sound of breaking glass. They could see that the windshield, made of safety-glass, had shattered into a million pieces, though it had not come out of the frame.

Later, as the ice melted, they touched the window. To their surprise, it was still completely smooth on the outside, though shattered on the inside.

How many ministers maintain a smooth, polished exterior, pretending nothing is wrong, that everything is glorious and under control? Yet, how many people know that, inwardly, their hearts and private worlds are shattered? To be seen as successful, Spirit-filled, and self-controlled, they feel they must maintain a smooth image. Yet, inside, they feel they are dying. To whom can they reveal their hurt? Would their congregations be surprised, or worse, would their congregations reject them?

Sometimes, those secrets are concealed from those who know him best, skillfully covered over by posturing and pretense. His best friends, his secretary, his staff, and even his spouse don't know, so carefully does he shield those areas from others.

His silent hurts might be as serious as the sins he battles. They might be as innocent as the wounds he bears, but he feels people wouldn't understand. There might be the fear that exposure would cost him his ministry. Many ministers have been taught they were not supposed to feel emotions like loneliness, for example. So he keeps up the deception and never gets the encouragement or help he needs. In addition, some ministers do not fully accept the private hurts they are experiencing, nor do they understand how their pain is shaping their attempts to minister. Successful pastors are healthy pastors, and healthy pastors are far more likely to build healthy churches. That health often comes after admitting the inner pain. However, a key question is, are they given the freedom to reveal their humanness?

These pages, my first effort at a book, were written after almost forty years as a pastor and dealing with other pastors. I once heard one of my spiritual heroes, Dr. Stephen Olford, say to a congregation, "You can't fool me, and I surely can't fool you." For the most part, that is true. When we serve a congregation, especially for a long time, pastor and people get to know a lot about each other. Still, some of us are busy playing the game, hiding the hurts within.

I know pastors and their struggles because I am one. I know church congregations because I serve one, the same one for almost thirty years. The people of my church have been remarkably patient in allowing me to express my humanity in many ways.

This book makes no claim to be a scholarly work. It is not a psychology textbook. It is completely pastoral in nature. The style is conversational: I hope not preachy, as though you and I were having a face-to-face meeting, revealing to each other our experiences.

I have been heavily influenced by things I have heard and read over the years about pastoral ministry. In most cases, I believe I have remembered and given credit to writers or speakers from whom I have learned. In some cases, I cannot remember. I hope these words will help some congregations, or, at least, some people in those congregations, by encouraging them to allow their pastors to be truly human. A pastor is not a superman without faults or feelings. He needs encouragement and the freedom to own up to his struggles without fear of rejection.

To be sure, some failings by ministers deserve action. But other struggles, like those spoken of here, should not be fatal to one's ministry, and in fact, deserve understanding and caring. Members of churches can provide that care to their pastors if they will. That will often require simple understanding.

Where people provide for their ministers the healing and encouragement they need, churches can profit greatly. By learning to extend graciousness and caring and listening to their leaders, churches may decide to extend those same responses to people outside the church. And to what a great harvest of souls that could eventually lead.

Perhaps, the following words of understanding and counsel, biblically based, will be helpful, as we seek together to be "... thoroughly furnished unto all good works." (2 Timothy 3:17b)

Chapter One

The Unspoken Agony of Ministry: Loneliness

2 Timothy 4:9-22

A man jumped into a taxi in New York City and told the driver where he wanted to go. As he pulled away from the curb, the driver handed the passenger a note, which read, "I'd rather you talk to me than tip me." Loneliness is one of our greatest fears and one of the most devastating situations we face.

It will come as a complete surprise to some that a minister would ever feel loneliness. There are always jangling telephones, with people on one end wanting to share his company. To some, it would seem that the minister would never lack companionship. Unfortunately, companionship itself often cannot fill the aching need for a close friend.

Then, there are the collegial relationships with other ministers in the area, or the larger denominational body. Surely, you think, they will all have a warm cooperative spirit, and everyone will work together for the good of the kingdom. That thought generally does not last long.

One day, the minister awakens to the realization that many people just want something from him. They do not necessarily want to be, or know how to be, a real friend. Some that give gifts do not

1

just want to bless him. They also want a special favor. And the congenial smiles often grow wan when two pastors are vying for the same new family in town as prospective church members. Having people around does not necessarily prevent loneliness. Sometimes, it only temporarily masks the loneliness.

Perhaps, there should be a distinction made between aloneness and loneliness. Aloneness is being without human companionship. Loneliness is being without genuine relationships. People can be alone without being lonely, and can be lonely without being alone. As Christians, we are never alone because we know the promise of God. But Christians can feel lonely, and if we are not careful, ministry can be hazardous to our real relationships.

I know of no group more plagued with loneliness than pastors and other "professional ministers." One pastor, in a time of profound struggle lamented, "It feels as though God had gone and taken all who matter with Him." I call loneliness the unspoken agony of the ministry because while it hurts desperately, we usually keep it quiet. We feel forced, by expectations of others, to live up to the image of "super-Christian," the all-sufficient holy person. In the minds of some, we're not supposed to need things ordinary people need.

But even the superstars in ministry get lonely. Think of those ministers with national or international exposure. Some need bodyguards to protect them from people. Yet, it was people they were once called to serve. Think how they must often crave just living a normal life with normal relationships. Celebrity status often carries with it the high price tag of intense loneliness. Think of that the next time you envy one of the media ministers. Paul the Apostle had achieved some degree of notoriety. So it is not surprising to hear him pour out his feelings of loneliness. Then we see the resources he had found to deal with his loneliness. Elizabeth Skoglund has written, "...to live beyond loneliness is a state for which kings would exchange their power and fortunes" (Elizabeth Skoglund, "Beyond Loneliness," Garden City, NY, Doubleday, 1980, p.118).

Most pastors don't have that much to exchange, but they would like to know how to live with their loneliness.

Loneliness Must Eventually Be Exposed

In verse nine, Paul writes to his younger protégée in the ministry, Timothy, "Do thy diligence to come shortly unto me...." Their relationship is interesting because Paul was obviously much older. Yet, he thought of Timothy as a colleague. That attitude from a seasoned minister is refreshing, indeed. When he was lonely, he longed for Timothy's company.

Verse twenty-one almost chokes with emotion, "Do your best to get here before winter." Paul asks for a few basic comforts of life. We would paraphrase his words, "Bring me books for reading, paper for writing, and my heavy coat." There were clear, practical reasons for wanting Timothy to hurry. Once winter set in, ships would be frozen in the ports and unable to sail. And Paul certainly needed his coat to survive winter. But I believe there is more here. Feel the apostle's mood as well as listening to his words.

Winter can be a bleak time, emotionally as well as physically. For those who suffer with the now recognized Seasonal Affective Disorder (S.A.D.), winter is an especially hard time. We are told it is at least partly because of diminished exposure to sunlight. One recommended treatment is exposure to full spectrum lighting while indoors. But a good friend would also help!

Depression and loneliness are cruel companions. Loneliness feels like winter in our souls. The Psalmist knew the feeling as he wrote in Psalm 102:7, "I watch, and am as a sparrow alone upon the house top." Have you ever seen a little brown sparrow sitting alone on the roof of your house on a gray day, shivering, and thought, "That is me?" I have, and if you are honest, so have you. Have you ever identified that empty feeling inside for what it is? Have you ever just admitted, "I am so lonely?"

3

There Are Many Reasons for Loneliness

In Paul's case, there was separation by geography. At this point, he was almost certainly in the dreaded Mamertine Prison in Rome awaiting his trial before Caesar. His real friends were far away. In his first court appearance, not one friend stood with him. As he extends greetings to his friends, you can hear his plaintive wish to be with them again. Some he had sent out on missionary tasks, like Crescens, Titus, and Tychichus. But there were other, darker reasons for his loneliness.

There was abandonment.

Paul specifically mentions Demas. Once a trusted friend and co-worker, because of a (love for) "this present world," Demas had abandoned Paul. So, add to the mix, disappointment. We have all known the frustration of seeing people we have discipled and worked with, grow spiritually, then fall away and desert us. It is hard not to take that personally. That creates feelings of loneliness.

There was attack.

We have these intriguing words, "Alexander the coppersmith did me much evil." He goes on to say, "for he hath greatly withstood our words." The only persons in ministry who never experience attack are either those in their first week on the job, those who make no efforts to lead, or those who never take a stand for anything. I have been told that my grandfather said, "The only way to avoid criticism is to say nothing, do nothing, and be nothing." Just being faithful and obedient to the Lord invites attack when people set themselves against the Lord and against our ministry. Being attacked certainly can create feelings of loneliness.

We are certainly not alone in those feelings. Jesus knew all this pain. He was abandoned by his friends in his hour of need. He saw countless people he helped, and whom he thought were his true friends, leave. Who can doubt that Jesus felt loneliness, when, as John 6:66 records, "from that time many of his disciples went back and walked no more with him." He was attacked with lies at his trial. The cross was the ultimate symbol of isolation. He hung there alone. The cross was the ultimate mark of what people were willing to do to those who simply followed God. The Son felt isolated from the Father as he hung on the cross. How else do you explain, "Eloi, Eloi, lama sabachthani" (Mark 15:34). Jesus was certainly attacked and cut off from both His friends and His Father. Yet He bore it all willingly.

There are also many other causes of loneliness that you and I know well.

Leadership itself comes with the weight of loneliness.

The leader is responsible for decisions and counsel that affect people's lives. There are certain matters in which the church looks to the pastor. As much as he might like to shift the responsibility to others, he cannot. That burden, alone, makes us feel lonely.

Much of the minister's work is done in isolation from others.

He spends hours in the study, the prayer room, and the counseling room, much of that time, alone.

Loneliness can be created by keeping confidences.

Things he hears may rock him to his soul, but he can't tell anyone, many times, not even his spouse.

Loneliness can be created by his own questions for God.

He leaves the hospital room, or the scene of an accident, and has his own life or death questions. "Do I believe what I just shared with them? If I should face the same thing, would I face it with joy? Why did such tragedy happen to a person like this? Lord, where are You in this? Will I be the next one to get cancer? Who will pastor me?" He has all those silent questions, but often thinks he is not supposed to voice them, because, of all people, he is supposed to model "perfect faith". That may not seem like loneliness to others, but it is one of the most intense forms of loneliness.

There are geographical factors in loneliness.

5

Many of us are separated by miles from our best friends. We see them only at denominational meetings. Unfortunately, the relationships we do have with other ministers are often artificial at worst, or superficial at best. It is tragic, but when preachers get together, they often don't listen as friends or support each other as friends. One-upmanship is in the air. Who has the biggest numbers or the greatest victories? If you didn't have a wonderful Sunday, if your church didn't meet the budget or see dozens saved, the Monday morning Minister's Conference can seem like the loneliest place on earth. You feel that everyone is looking at you saying, *What's wrong with you? Why can't you produce the results?*

There is a pastor I have always wanted to know. We have a lot in common. I respect him greatly. But when we are together and I share a personal burden or struggle, he always tops me. The same is true when I share a personal victory. When I talk, he is obviously thinking of what he is going to say next instead of listening, because he constantly interrupts me. I hope he does not treat his people that hastily. We will likely never be close friends because he sends the message he does not have the time for me.

Doctrinal differences and competitive spirits create loneliness.

Let's face it. Pastors often feel like competitors. And people don't help the situation with the current fad of church-hopping. I will admit that I have occasionally heightened my own sense of loneliness by also feeling resentment toward another pastor because of a bigger, more successful program that attracted people I thought should have joined my church.

Church members often compare their pastor to the big boys on television. Every week, they see packed churches and hear professional music and the most gifted preaching in America. Their reaction is often, "Why can't you be more like my TV pastor?" TV ministries can be a good thing, but in people's minds, their pastor may often come out short in comparison. They never stop to think that their media minister will never sit by their bedside when they are sick, or perform their daughter's wedding ceremony, or do the most of the other things that require a faithful pastor's presence.

There is loneliness in failure.

You have just preached a bad sermon. You know it, and you know people know it. Someone will always say, "Good sermon, Pastor." But you know they are only being polite. Few people will be so bold with their shepherd as to say "Bad sermon." But in a way, you wish they would, and then try to comfort and encourage you. The fact that you know you did less than your best yet there will be no comfort, produces loneliness. Who *does* comfort the pastor when he has failed in his responsibilities?

There is loneliness when relationships at home are not good.

Home is the ultimate place people can feel lonely though not alone. You are struggling in your marriage. You are experiencing the heartbreak of a child in rebellion. You know no human being can make it go away, but you would like to tell someone. Yet, who?

There is always that inevitable person who trots out. (1 Timothy 3:4-5)

"One that ruleth well his own house, having his children in subjection with all gravity; (For if a man know not how to rule his own house, how shall he take care of the church of God?)"

Then they say, "If you can't manage your own house and keep your children *under control*, maybe you are not fit to be our pastor." Talk about judgmentalism! So, you tell no one lest you bear the brunt of rebuke.

Anger causes loneliness.

You didn't get the raise you needed. You were unfairly criticized. People in the church are unresponsive. Pastors get angry. Anger drives people away. But even if you don't show it, anger that settles in for a long stay creates self-pity, and self-pity creates unbelievably intense feelings of loneliness.

7

Superiority feelings create loneliness.

The nature of our work is such that people treat us a little differently. There is the title "Reverend." We are the "professional holy man." Some think that because of his high calling the pastor must be unapproachable, so they shy away from relationships the pastor might welcome. Sometimes, we would like to be thought of as just a regular person, but there is also the danger that we can begin to enjoy and expect special treatment. That only increases the problem of loneliness.

We don't get a lot of help from people in the congregation in dealing with loneliness, especially if we don't acknowledge our loneliness, ask for help, and allow it. Many people believe we are supposed to be self-sufficient, or, at least, that Jesus alone is supposed to be sufficient for us.

Don't misunderstand, I believe in the total sufficiency of the Lord Jesus Christ. But He wants to supply many of our emotional needs through human companionship and genuine relationships as He does for everyone else. The problem comes when we begin to think of ourselves as the super-pastor. There is so much of what can be called "acting" in the ministry, and it cuts us off from the relationships we need.

Here, the problem gets sticky. Many of us were told from the beginning of our ministry, "Don't make close friendships in the church. People will think you are playing favorites." So, we can't make friends with other ministers because of competition. We can't make friends within the church because of favoritism. We don't reveal our hurts or weaknesses to colleagues because we fear exposure. Where do we turn?

Paul faced much of this as well. It is important to see one of the first steps he took in dealing with his loneliness. At least it was a step that prevented the compounding of the problem. He displayed *a forgiving spirit*. Verse sixteen displays the graciousness of Paul in the face of abandonment and attack, "I pray God that it may not be laid to their charge."

Paul did not compound the problem with resentment, which leads to self-pity, which increases the isolation and loneliness. Instead, he forgave. We will deal with this unspoken need in Chapter Two. If loneliness is the unspoken agony of the ministry, resentment may well be the most common, unspoken sin of ministry. When our leadership is rejected, we get angry. Anger leads to bitterness. Bitterness only heightens the feelings of alienation in us, even if we think we don't show it outwardly (which we often do). Bitterness damages relationships. The fruit of the Holy Spirit in us is patience and the ability to forgive.

Once again, Jesus embodied forgiveness. From the cross, He cried, "Father, forgive them…." Forgiveness is not the total cure for loneliness. It is, however, a start, because it deals with the resentment that builds walls around your life and isolates you. Where did Paul turn in his loneliness?

There are Ways to Deal with Loneliness

It is important to deal with loneliness. You can live through aloneness, but you will be destroyed by loneliness. Loneliness eats at the heart. Loneliness makes us feel that no one cares about us and that things will never get any better. Loneliness makes us feel there must be something wrong with us that drives people away or makes them not want to be with us. All these may be lies our spirit is telling us, but they seem convincing, at least at the moment, and we do tend to believe them. So, how do we deal with loneliness?

There is the resource of the faithful presence of the Lord.

Paul says, "The Lord stood with me." Do you ever think how wonderful it is that the believer never has to insult the integrity of the Lord by saying, "Be with me"? Even in his aloneness, the

9

Lord Jesus said, "I am not alone" (John 8:16). How marvelous are promises like these?

> "...and be content with such things as ye have: for he hath said, I will never leave thee, nor forsake thee." (Hebrews 13:5)

> "For the mountains shall depart and the hills be removed; but my kindness shall not depart from thee, neither shall the covenant of my peace be removed, saith the Lord that hath mercy on thee." (Isaiah 54:10)

We may occasionally be without companionship, but we are never without relationship, in the ultimate sense. Jesus said, "I am with you always...". (Matthew 28:20)

> "Mine eyes are ever toward the Lord; for he shall pluck my feet out of the net. Turn thee unto me, and have mercy upon me; for I am desolate and afflicted. The troubles of my heart are enlarged: o bring thou me out of my distresses. Look upon mine affliction and my pain; and forgive all my sins." (Psalm 25:15-18)

When we are in our lonely desert times, and fix our eyes on the Lord, when we recognize His fullness and love, our loneliness will be swallowed up in the wonder of His comforting care.

> "The Lord is nigh unto them that are of a broken heart; and saveth such as be of a contrite spirit." (Psalm 34:18)

In the midst of the darkness of loneliness, keep reading the Word of comfort until you can believe it and see its' true light. Our greatest resource for dealing with loneliness is on the inside, since the origin of loneliness is also on the inside. Our relationship to Him is absolutely secure, and His love for us is absolutely unconditional. But how many of us have preached the comfort of Christ, the abiding presence of Christ, and the unconditional love of Christ for others, yet not rested in those truths for ourselves? Trust Him! He has not deserted you no matter what your pained heart tells you!

How much more plain does he need to be than in Matthew 28:20 where He says, "I am with you always." When you feel that your security has been ripped away from you, can you believe that the Lord of love enfolds you and brings you into His place of security—His heart?

There is also *the comforting presence of friends* as a resource for our times of loneliness. Paul's theme is found in his words to Timothy, "Come shortly unto me." He has Luke, he asks for Timothy and John Mark. It is always right to rely on the Lord's faithful presence and strength. But sometimes, we all need help that has skin on. It is true that some have been taught not to make friendships within the church lest jealousy arise. But what right thinking person is jealous of his doctor's friends, or his dentist's friends? He doesn't own his pastor any more than he owns his doctor. The truth is, some members of the congregation may be waiting for the opportunity to walk into their pastor's heart with legitimate friendship, if he will allow them to.

Beyond what Paul has revealed, are there other answers? Some ministers, I am sorry to say, take the wrong approach. Rather than avail themselves of God's resources, they look for answers elsewhere.

Some *become more gregarious but have no depth to their relationships.* It is probably better to have a few close or deep relationships than many which are only superficial. Superficial relationships only temporarily divert our attention from our feelings. Deep relationships satisfy.

Some ministers *spend money*. There is research showing that many people whose spending and personal debt are out of control spend the most when they are feeling lonely and depressed.

Also, the sad truth is, some ministers *turn to practices and habits they know are wrong*, the kind that would shock their congregations. They enter a private world of fantasy as an escape from loneliness. Gambling, drugs, alcohol, pornography, and sexual affairs claims some ministers, but are rarely acknowledged until they are discovered to everyone's embarrassment.

So what other proper approaches are there to dealing with loneliness?

Perhaps most important, *major on your relationship at home*. If things are wrong there, things will never be right in your ministry. Your spouse is a place of refuge. Your spouse literally has the arms of comfort physically and emotionally. Do whatever is required to see there are the qualities of depth, wholeness, and welcome in your marriage.

If isolation is a frequent reality in your ministry, *learn the benefits of isolation*. Instead of thinking "loneliness," think "solitude". Solitude gives you more time to focus on developing your inner life and on the enabling presence of the Holy Spirit. Meditate on Scripture, re-examine your life. Strengthen your personal walk with God. Become more of a prayer warrior. Change your prospective on your circumstances. Some of the greatest devotional writings and most significant revival moments of the church have come from those who have known how to use their solitude well.

In a place and time of solitude when no other voices are heard, you are more open to hear God's voice. Remember that even Jesus, when pressed by noisy and demanding crowds often *sought* a place of refuge and prayer to refocus His life and ministry. Do you and I have any less need for that? In solitude, we learn things about ourselves. Some are pleasing. Some are disturbing. But learning the things that are in our heart is essential if we are to experience fully the enjoyment and empowering of the Spirit.

Make the best use of your time. Loneliness tends to paralyze us. Loneliness makes us sit and do nothing. Instead, care for your physical health, eat right, exercise. Study and write. Paul asked for books and writing paper! If Paul had not been isolated in prison, he would have been in the Coliseum or the marketplace preaching. So God left him in prison alone, and we got part of the New Testament! Paul used his time well. If you can't be where you think the action is, create action where you are.

Minimize the hurt you feel. Don't rehearse your loneliness over and over again. Don't ever let your praying degenerate into, "Lord, I am so lonely." Focus on the positives about your circumstances. Especially focus on the promise of the Lord's presence.

Empathize with others.

Instead of always praying, "Lord, send me somebody to be *my* friend," pray "Lord, lead me to somebody to whom I can *be* a friend." Love is perhaps the best human antidote to loneliness.

When God brings someone into your life with whom friendship is a possibility, drop the piousness and pretense and the hurriedness that prevent friendships. Drop the feelings of competition. Learn to listen and encourage each other, or the friendship will never become anything more than superficial.

Consider an accountability group.

Choose people who can be absolutely trusted to listen, care, and keep confidences. Choose people who are mature enough, wise enough, and healthy enough to encourage, challenge, and even confront when needed in a spirit of love, not judgmentalism.

If the problem behind much of your loneliness is that you feel your life has been wasted and your ministry ineffective, consider this: It takes a great deal of selective and deliberate blindness to believe that you have been totally ineffective. You may not have the numbers some others have. But try measuring your successes in smaller ways. You were faithful to that family in a devastating time and they love you for it. Your ministry to that woman in crisis resulted in her salvation. Do those seem like small successes? Possibly they do. But they are successes nonetheless. Self-pity that comes from comparison creates devastating loneliness. But you isolate yourself if you allow yourself to believe that you have been a failure.

You may already understand that with ministry comes loneliness. It is also true that out of loneliness can come ministry. When we discover the reality of God's faithful love, our approach to others in pain will also be with a new compassion and understanding.

Dr. Harold Ivan Smith has written that on his deathbed, Revolutionary War traitor, Benedict Arnold was asked if he needed anything. He gasped, "Yes, a friend." We have all found ourselves there. We identify with the dungeon talk of Paul. Our prison may not be a grimy, stoned-walled cell like his. We sit in a nice study every day. Our chains may be responsibilities and disappointments, not clanking metal. But the feelings of loneliness are the same.

In our times of loneliness, there is a Friend that sticks closer than a brother. His name is Jesus Christ. Let Him help you walk through and even conquer your loneliness as you refocus on Him in prayer, and as you reach out to other lonely people around you.

Chapter Two

The Unspoken Sin of the Ministry: Resentment

The following story is true. The names have been changed to protect the guilty.

Pastor James had been in the ministry almost five years. He was in his third month at his present church. He knew mistakes in judgment were common in young ministers. However, he had always considered that he had exceptional judgment for his age and experience. The moment he spoke the harsh words to the chairman of the official church board, though, he knew he had made a bad mistake.

In his mind, the chairman had engaged in a raw exercise of power. It was an action the pastor felt was completely unwarranted, and, in fact, not allowed by the church constitution. The angry pastor summoned the chairman, Mr. Evans, to his study, and reprimanded him. Mr. Evans looked stunned at first. Then, he went on the offensive. The color rose to his cheeks. He stated that no pastor has ever dared to speak to him that way. Both men spoke sharply to each other for almost fifteen minutes.

Pastor James, who at first felt completely justified, now realized he had blundered. In fact, he knew he was guilty of the same attempted exercise of power. He also sensed he had made a dangerous enemy. Walls of hostility went up on both sides.

Over the next few months, Mr. Evans seemed determined to embarrass his pastor. He openly threatened to leave his church. In a board meeting, he asked that the pastor be publicly censured for an especially strong sermon.

For his part, Pastor James went out of his way to avoid Mr. Evans. He dreaded board meetings. Even a written message, "Call Mr. Evans," made his heart pound with nervousness. He knew the chairman could make his life miserable, or even have him terminated.

In his mind, he increasingly resented the treatment he was receiving. He felt this leadership of the staff and his freedom of the pulpit had been unfairly challenged. Neither man had ever acknowledged his own wrongdoing nor sought forgiveness. Nor had either forgiven the other for what were obvious sins.

Over the next three years, resentment of Mr. Evans grew in the pastor's heart. He sought every way possible to go around stated church procedures in order to avoid dealing with the chairman. He felt Mr. Evans was against him and his vision for the church. He felt Mr. Evans would do anything to block his leadership. He believed Mr. Evans was undercutting him to the other church members.

He was probably correct in all three assessments. But his personal ministry to Mr. Evans was non-existent. In his attempt to justify his own actions, Pastor James was behaving in a most un-pastoral way. Though he did not start the situation, the pastor knew he had not responded in a Christ-like way. Holding onto resentment and anger toward Mr. Evans caused the pastor to view him and his close friends in a completely negative way.

Years later, reflecting on his spirit and actions, Pastor James acknowledged his sin. However, by then, the broken relationship between the two men appeared to have deteriorated beyond solution.

Sounds familiar? The situation may have been different, but virtually every pastor or church member reading this can remember some situation or some conflict that produced resentment.

It has been said that resentment is not a primary emotion. Fear and frustration are primary emotions which lead to anger. Anger, when stored in the heart, becomes resentment. Resentment, which some call bitterness, is the inward nurturing of feelings of personal hurt. It is often accompanied by a desire for revenge, or, at least, a desire that the other person experience serious negative consequences for his or her actions.

After years of knowing and being with hundreds of fellow ministers, I notice now a higher degree of frustration, anger, and resentment among many ministers than before. I see it causing serious consequences in their relationships and their ministries. Many of those consequences are, I believe, traceable to the failure to resolve buried resentments. But often, the issue of resentment in the minister's life is never spoken of at all.

Do ministers need reminding about the danger of resentment, or the importance of forgiving? They preach to and counsel people in their congregations about those very issues. Surely, they would heed their own counsel.

The truth is, ministers do need reminding. The reason is summed up in one word: "humanness". Ministers experience resentment, like anyone else, because they are human. "Humanness" may be the explanation for resentment, but it is never the justification for resentment.

All believers have been given the challenge of a "renewed mind" (Romans 12:1-2). All believers have been given the power of grace and the dynamic of the Holy Spirit to deal with sin. That includes the sins of the heart and spirit such as resentment.

The minister may not speak of his resentment for several reasons:

- He doesn't even recognize the presence of resentment in his life.
- He feels justified in the feelings he holds because of how badly he was treated.
- He recognizes that resentment is sin, but is ashamed to admit it to others.
- Virtually every day brings circumstances which can breed resentment.
- The pastor gives his best in the pulpit, but he is compared to a successful TV pastor, and people whisper that he is "just not a good preacher."
- Expectation levels are so high, he feels constantly drained.
- Because of feeling strapped financially, he feels the church must be praying, "Lord, you keep him humble, we'll keep him poor."
- His vision for the church is rejected.
- He plans a special day of emphasis, but the crowds are small.
- A confidence spoken to a friend is violated.
- The congregation does not share their pastor's enthusiasm for a new ministry.

Obviously, there are many more circumstances taken so personally that resentment is the result.

Learning to acknowledge resentment is only part of what must be done. More will be said later about how churches can help their ministers through this issue. But the real answer to resentment is found in the power of forgiveness. Forgiveness can be practiced whether or not the church ever learns of or understands the struggle of their minister with resentment. For forgiveness that brings healing is an intensely personal issue.

Forgiveness of others is a subject being increasingly addressed even in the secular world. This writer first began to notice the trend after reading a book by Dr. Lewis Smedes, entitled, *Forgive and*

Forget: Healing the Hurts We Don't Deserve (Harper and Row, 1984). Other books followed, by non-Christian writers. Those I saw, however, had an amazingly Christian sound to them.

Who Needs to Forgive?

People who have been hurt by rejection, betrayal, divorce, and violence need to forgive. People who feel ignored by those who are supposed to love them need to forgive. Ministers who feel unsupported and overburdened need to forgive. Ministers who have invested years and energy in serving a church only to see very few results need to forgive. Those who have been lied about or forcibly terminated need to forgive.

A critical issue here, is, what constitutes forgiveness? Many people never approach the matter of forgiveness because they misunderstand what forgiveness is. Forgiveness in no sense implies pretending something did not happen, or that it did not matter. Forgiveness is certainly not delayed retaliation, keeping something in the back of the mind until we need it. Forgiveness is letting the burden of the past go. Forgiveness is willingly accepting a person who wronged us on the basis of love and caring, instead of dealing with them on the basis of what they did. Forgiveness is learning to separate the person from his or her offense against us. Forgiveness is surrendering to God the aim of getting personal satisfaction for something done to us by *continually holding the other person guilty*.

Resentment Destroy Us

Few things have such power to ruin our lives, our joy, our attitude, and our days as resentment. During the five-month long unsuccessful battle my pastor- father fought with pancreatic cancer, I kept a journal of all my experiences and feelings as I helped care for him. By the graciousness of our church, I spent two or three days each week at his bedside and wrote mostly after he went to sleep. Besides the experiences and emotions I was facing, I also wrote about many experiences of the past, not all of them pleasant.

Though my father had tried to shield me from the knowledge of many of the unpleasant parts of ministry he had endured in the past, I knew he had waded through the deep waters of opposition and mistreatment. In the summer of 2004, after his death, I finally summoned the courage to put on paper my personal feelings about people I had formerly admired who had treated him badly. It had been more than forty years before and in another state, but up to that point, I had not allowed myself to face my strong negative emotions about some of them. After all, they were people and leaders I had been taught to respect and did respect. I began to realize I had very deep-seated feelings of resentment toward them.

One of my first clues about how I felt about them was probably the pain in my stomach. I literally got a burning sensation in my stomach whenever I thought of them. My day turned bleak and black as I rehearsed the wrong done to my father. I also discovered that when I was able to come to the point of forgiveness by faith, I felt more relief than when I took the antacid tablets I constantly carried. It was amazing the relief a forgiving spirit brought.

I am certain Apostle Paul knew nothing of antacid tablets, and I am equally certain he knew the cure for resentment and its negative effects on the spirit, mind, and body.

Perhaps, that is why he wrote in Ephesians 4:30-32,

"And grieve not the Holy Spirit of God, whereby ye are sealed unto the day of redemption. Let all bitterness and wrath, and anger, and clamor, and evil speaking, be put away from you, with all malice. And be ye kind one to another, tenderhearted, forgiving one another, even as God for Christ's sake hath forgiven you."

Paul had known resentment from several sides. He felt it and held it because of his hatred for the followers of Jesus before his conversion, while he was still known as Saul of Tarsus. He had allowed his resentment to cause his participation in the murder of at least one follower, the noble deacon Stephen.

Saul had undoubtedly caused some resentment because of his treatment of other believers. On a rough country road, his heart had been changed by the entrance of Jesus Christ. However, that also caused Paul to once again become the object of resentment—this time from the opposite side, his own countrymen. They resented his having become a follower of "The Way" himself. If anyone could ever speak with authority on the subject of resentment, it was Paul. He asserted, "Don't let bitterness (resentment) win you. Instead you win over it by forgiveness and tenderheartedness toward each other." To ministers today, many of whom have been truly hurt, Paul would say, "If you want to please the Holy Spirit and be used by Him, which *all* believers should, don't cause Him pain and negate His power within by holding onto resentment."

The Greek word for bitterness in Ephesians 4:31 means "smoldering resentment, brooding over a grudge that keeps irritating." It can even mean, "Constant feelings of animosity toward someone." Before it escalades into shouting, quarreling, and just plain meanness, deal with it. Deal with it by forgiveness.

What Is Forgiveness?

There are several New Testament words for "forgiveness". *Aphiemi* means "to send away," or "put away." The idea is to release from guilt a person now being held as guilty. When a person has wronged us, some of us hold them guilty. We may say we forgive them, to ourselves and others. We may even associate with them. But, mentally, we write an IOU, and say, "You owe me. I will make you pay, some day, some way." Then our life begins to revolve around the plans to make that happen. The offense is always on our mind. We think of it with bitterness each time we see the person. Forgiveness says, "I'll cancel the debt. You no longer owe it. I'm tearing up the IOU."

Charizomai, another New Testament word, means "to grant favor, unconditionally." It is from the same root word for "grace", which describes how God treats us when we place our faith in Jesus Christ. He does not give us what we *do* deserve. Instead, He chooses to give us what we do *not* deserve. Instead of condemning us, He accepts us. The idea is to always be ready to extend graciousness to one who has wronged us.

Then, there is *apolyo*. This means forgiveness in the sense of "letting something pass by." This is just letting it go, choosing not to be offended. Some people, including some ministers, not only need the ability to forgive, they need the determination not to be so demonstrative of their feelings that they virtually dare anyone to hurt them. Some people are so sensitive; they let themselves be offended by almost anything. It would be funny if not sad.

I will be the first to admit it can be hard for a minister to forgive when it is the business of the kingdom at stake. When you believe you know the "secret" to your church growing and the people in the power structures won't listen to or support you and your effort, it is easy to feel justified in holding onto resentment. But the pastor's resentments, however defensible they may feel, will, in time, only cripple him and further stifle the work of the church.

There are many other New Testament passages about forgiveness. Jesus said in Matthew 5:7, "Blessed are the merciful, for they shall obtain mercy." One interpretation of that is, "Happy are those who extend and express mercy in forgiving those who wrong them."

In the Model Prayer, Jesus taught us to pray, "Father...forgive us our debts, *as we* forgive our debtors." The only portion of that prayer on which Jesus made immediate further commentary was verse twelve. He amplified His words in Matthew 6:14, "...for if you forgive men their trespasses, your heavenly Father will also forgive you; but if ye forgive not men their trespasses, neither will your Father forgive your trespasses."

All ministers have preached that, but have we practiced it as well, and realized the liberating power of forgiveness in our lives? I do not, for a minute, believe that God's forgiveness comes with strings attached, a sort of conditional forgiveness. I do believe Jesus is teaching that if we choose to live, characterized by a continual pattern of unforgiveness, that may be a loud witness that we ourselves are not experiencing God's forgiveness of us.

Jesus emphasized the ongoing nature of forgiveness in Matthew 18:21-22,

> "Then came Peter to him and said, Lord how oft shall my brother sin against me, and I forgive him? Till seven times? Jesus saith unto him, I say not unto thee, until seven times; but until seventy times seven."

Jesus was certainly not advocating "keeping score" and cutting off forgiveness upon the four hundred ninety-first offense. I Corinthians 13:5 notes, "...(love) thinketh no evil." That means, love does not keep a record of wrongs. Jesus spoke metaphorically. "Forgive so much you lose count."

Then Jesus told a memorable story.

> "Therefore is the kingdom of heaven likened unto a certain king, which would take account of his servants. And when

he had begun to reckon, one was brought unto him, which owed him ten thousand talents. But foreasmuch as he had not to pay, his lord commanded him to be sold, and his wife, and children, and all that he had, and payment to be made. The servant therefore fell down, and worshipped him, saying, Lord have patience with me, and I will pay thee all. Then the Lord of that servant was moved with compassion, and loosed him, and forgave the debt. But the same servant went out, and found one of his fellow servants, which owed him a hundred pence: and he laid hands on him, and took him by the throat, saying, Pay me that thou owest. And his fellow servant fell down at his feet, and besought him, saying, Have patience with me and I will pay thee all. And he would not: but went and cast him into prison, till he should pay him the debt. So when his fellow servants saw what was done, they were very sorry, and came and told unto their lord all that was done. Then his lord, after that he had called him, said unto him, O thou wicked servant, I forgave thee all that debt, because thou desiredst me: shouldest not thou also have had compassion on thy fellow servant, even as I had pity on thee? And his lord was wroth, and delivered him to the tormentors, til he should pay all that was due unto him. So likewise shall my Heavenly Father do also unto you, if ye from your hearts forgive not every one his brother their trespasses" (Matthew 18:21-35)

Jesus' basic message was, we are all more debtors than creditors. It took incredible grace for God to give His Son for our sins. If we have trusted Him, God has completely forgiven us. How could we dare to hold onto wrongs done to us, when God covenanted, in Christ, to release all charges against us? Debtors have no business cherishing bad debts against them.

Grace is a radical concept. That God would offer to forgive those who did not deserve it, on the basis of His Son's sacrifice, is remarkable. It is seen by some as radical to preach it. It is far more radical to practice it. Few ministers fail to preach the grace of God for salvation. But do they exercise the power of grace in forgiving those who stand in their way, disappoint them, frustrate them, or wound them? The preaching of grace will ring hollow in the life of a minister who does not practice it. And, frankly, the experience of grace will never be complete or totally satisfying as long as old scores remain on the books.

So Why Won't We Forgive?

Many of us are experts at offering excuses for not forgiving. One of the most often heard, and, honestly, one of the most understandable is, *"If I forgive, that means I am justifying what they did.* What they did to me was too awful. It was inexcusable. If I forgive them, I am saying, 'I understand, it's okay, it doesn't matter.'"

Unless you have been the victim of extreme brutality or cruelty, don't dismiss this excuse lightly. One who has been violated sexually, or lied about until his or her reputation was permanently ruined, may easily feel forgiveness is letting the person off too lightly. Is there a pastor reading these words who has seen his life seemingly destroyed because of the underserved attack of someone? You know how easily this reasoning comes.

But forgiveness is not excusing what someone did. It is not okay. It does matter what happened. Forgiveness is not justifying what they did. It is saying, "I'll let the past go, I'll let the present be, I'll let the future get back to normal." As long as we refuse to forgive, we are living in the past. Forgiving is saying, "I will not let this event continue to hurt. It hurt me once when it happened. It is still hurting me because I am giving it a life of its own through this resentment, and *that* is doing me even more harm. I will not let this control me. I will not be a victim. I will not be a prisoner of resentment."

Resentment will have many more than the proverbial nine lives if we allow it. All people, including ministers, can come to the point of saying, "It wasn't okay, but I will no longer be at the mercy of this event in my past. I will choose to forgive."

Another common excuse is, *"They didn't ask my forgiveness."* Ultimately, however, that is not the issue. You are not responsible for them. You are only responsible for you. A resentful spirit is our responsibility, whether or not they have asked for forgiveness.

Sometimes, those who hurt us are not aware of the damage they have done. How can they ask forgiveness? They will likely not respond well to our telling them they wronged us. There is a dynamic Christlikeness about one who, in the throes of pain, activates the power of God to forgive. Do these two prayers sound familiar?

"Then said Jesus, Father forgive them; for they know not what they do." (Luke 23:34a)

And he (Stephen) kneeled down, and cried with a loud voice, Lay not this sin to their charge. And when he had said this, he fell asleep." (Acts 7:60)

No one reading this has been crucified or stoned to death. This was mistreatment at its highest. The tormentors never asked for forgiveness. But both the Lord Jesus and Deacon Stephen offered a forgiving spirit.

Still others maintain that resentment feels like the only way to get a measure of justice or revenge. They know it is not, but it feels that way. To be mistreated is to feel like a helpless victim. To hold onto resentment feels like a small measure of power over someone else. A resentful spirit masquerades as a defiant and unconquerable spirit. In reality, a resentful spirit is a shriveling spirit.

The one who holds onto resentment is only hurting himself. Holding resentment is like putting a deadly coral snake inside your shirt, or inviting a serial killer home. You will be the victim.

Besides, no one has yet put any of us in charge of rendering ultimate justice or vengeance. That task resides with God. These are powerful words from Paul, once the one who held resentment, then the one who was the object of resentment.

> "Recompense to no man evil for evil. Provide things honest in the sight of all men. If it be possible, as much as lieth in you, live peaceably with all men. Dearly beloved, avenge not yourselves, but rather give place unto wrath, for it is written, Vengeance is mine, I will repay, saith the Lord. Therefore if thine enemy hunger, feed him; if he thirst, give him drink; for in so doing thou shalt heap coals of fire upon his head. Be not overcome of evil, but overcome evil with good." (Romans 12:17-21)

Forgive and Forget?

I confess that I once naively said, "Forgive and forget. If you are not forgetting, you are not forgiving." I think I now understand how wrong and even cruel that was. Biologically, our unpleasant memories are not destroyed by the act of deliberate forgiveness. Forgiveness is being able to think of the person without being dominated by the emotion. That may take time, and much forgiving. It may take help from a counselor. But it can happen.

Has anyone ever said to you, "God forgets our sins when He forgives us"? That is not exactly what the Bible says. Isaiah 43:25 is certainly a blessed promise, filled with gifts of hope and relief for our guilty hearts as it states,

"I, even I, am he that blotteth out thy transgressions for mine own sake, and will not remember thy sins."

But the idea expressed actually means, "I will never charge you with that sin again once I blot it out. I will not hold it against you." Thank God for that promise, but it does not mean the memory is eradicated. If we *could* remember, biologically, sins once forgiven, yet God could not, we would be able to do something God is not capable of doing. God says, "I will not bring it up again." That is the pattern for our forgiveness.

Some people are "quick forgivers." Others take more time. But our hearts should be filled with the calm of forgiveness instead of with the torment of resentment.

Reverend Walter Everett displayed the ability to forgive when forgiveness was tough.

In 1987, Michael Carlucci shot Reverend Everett's son, William, while both he and William were drunk. He pleaded guilty to manslaughter and was sentenced to five years in prison. At the sentencing, Michael Carlucci apologized for what he had done and this touched Everett.

Everett began to correspond with Carlucci. After Carlucci had served 2 ½ years in prison, Everett testified for him at his parole hearing and Carlucci was released. On Saturday, November 12, 1994, Everett officiated Carlucci's wedding.

Reverend Everett explained, "I had known people whose loved ones had been murdered, but years afterward, they still seemed consumed by the anger and the hatred. I didn't want that to happen to me."

So he practiced forgiveness, even when forgiveness was tough.

Honestly, has any reader been that wronged? Have you forgiven that much?

Abundant Motives for Forgiving

One motive for forgiving is found in Ephesians 4:30 where Paul said that we "grieve the Holy Spirit of God" when we hold onto resentment. Bitterness breaks the heart of God the Spirit. The Spirit is our source of spiritual life and growth. Resentment prevents growth by blocking the Spirit's reconciling, comforting, and encouraging work in us.

It is amazing that some ministers, and, indeed, others, can genuinely attempt to be so righteous in other areas of life, yet so blind or so stubborn about this one. They claim deep experiences with the blessed Holy Spirit, but go on ignoring or justifying a bitter human spirit.

To repeat an earlier theme, we are to forgive because we, ourselves, have been forgiven by God. The degree to which we have been forgiven by Him is far greater that the degree to which we have been wronged by others. Wrongs done to us are small change compared to the huge debt we owed to God, which he forgave by the blood of His Son.

If we do not forgive, resentment will ruin our lives, our attitude, and even our health. Ever since reading the book by Dr. S. I. McMillan, *None of These Diseases* (F. H. Revell, 1963), I have been acutely aware of how related bitterness and resentment are to high blood pressure and stress related illness.

There are also consequences directly related to the minister's influence and work, which often are completely unconsidered. Resentment may feel like a measure of power or control over someone, but it always backfires.

Resentment will warp the minister's judgment and counsel. Pastor James, mentioned above, found that attitudes of vindictiveness were beginning to creep into his counsel. He actually recognized one day that he was advising people to try to strike back at people who wronged them, not physically, but in other ways. He was spreading the poison of resentment.

Resentment will eventually show in the minister's face, voice, and body language. The congregation may well sense hostility and strain in their minister. No one will long follow or listen to an angry pastor, except other angry people who will create angry churches that will be of little use to the kingdom of God.

Resentment will distort one's teaching and preaching. Angry pastors often use their pulpit as a place to verbally and emotionally beat their people. The pulpit may be used as a place to vent his own resentments instead of proclaiming the Good News that heals. Angry pastors are often more interested in controlling people than enabling them to discover their freedom in Christ.

Resentment will destroy one's personal prayer life and spiritual growth. How could there be any doubt of that after reading 1 Peter 2:1-2:

> "Wherefore laying aside all malice, and all guile, and hypocrisies, and envies, and all evil speaking, as newborn babes, desire the sincere milk of the word, that ye may grow thereby."

Resentment may become generalized to the whole congregation. Perhaps it creates a sort of paranoia, but the minister who allows resentment to fester may begin to feel that it is not just the one person who is hurting him. He may begin to believe "they are all after me."

Resentment may blind the minister to even genuine efforts of the one who wronged him to repent and move toward him in love. Resentment can so distort our thinking and emotions that we are no longer willing to accept the possibility of restoration.

One of the subtle traps of resentment is that is it possessive. Resentment comes to shape our way of relating to people. When resentment becomes a pattern of life, we begin to expect to be hurt or rejected.

Resentment may make a minister reluctant or even unwilling to minister to the person who has wounded him, even in crisis. Psychologists have identified the "approach-avoidance syndrome" in such broken relationships. The nature of our calling says we shouldn't ignore them, so we are drawn to help (approach). Yet, because of resentment, we don't want to help (avoidance). It is only approaching that could help restore the relationship, but the heart can become unwilling. Of course, that leaves the minister open to charges of being cold and uncaring, certainly the death knell for his ministry.

Can Resentment be Justified?

What is so tragic is that many ministers pretentiously attempt to justify their resentment. Scripture can become a weapon piously wielded in the cause. More than one minister, suffering through attack or resistance, has trotted out Psalm 105:15,

"Touch not mine anointed, and do my prophets no harm."

That verse may first be used to intimidate people into never challenging him or his leadership ("Touch not"). Then, if he is still rejected or hurt, once again he refers to that verse so he can take comfort in the truth that he is "(God's) anointed; therefore, he must be justified in feeling so wounded. And, of course, he knows that God will judge the one who dares to challenge him. So, if God won't "let them off the hook," why should he?

As to the particular verse, it is virtually impossible to make it apply to today's clergy without doing serious damage to both text and context. It is God's warning to the nations and rulers of the world not to harm any of *all* of His people, who serve as "prophets". They all declare His goodness and glory to the world.

Forgiveness Takes Place in the Heart

Resentment does not respond to a simple 1-2-3 step activity. Forgiveness takes root in a heart that is prepared both by human choices and divine enablement. The person who focuses more on the marvel of divine love and grace and seeks for his heart to be immersed in the person of Christ will be more likely to forgive than the one who continually focuses on the mechanics of forgiving. Forgiveness may be more of an environment of the heart than an action. The heart is freed to forgive the more we focus on the enormous reality of our own forgiveness by Christ. As Adrian Rogers used to say, "Never get over being saved."

Forgiveness must become a lifestyle. Saturday night repentance of this or any sin in preparation for Sunday's duties is no substitute for the ongoing practice of forgiving and letting go of offenses against us. Having said that, however, there are some specifics that may help.

Do spiritual surgery. Separate the person from the offense. Make the commitment before Almighty God that what they did does not mean they are without worth. By grace, by faith, by a deliberate choice, release them from lasting guilt or indebtedness to you. Determine not to be controlled by resentment or be in bondage to anger.

Remember that emotions must not be the master here. Your emotions may not feel a sense of forgiveness. Forgive the person anyway! Emotions are followers. Forgive by conscious choice, and, in time, emotions will usually follow.

Forgiveness must then be demonstrated by meaningful action. Jesus was very specific in telling us how to deal with enemies, "Ye have heard that it hath been said, thou shalt love thy neighbor and hate thine enemy. But I say unto you, love your enemies, bless them that curse you, do good to them that hate you, and pray for them which despitefully use you, and persecute you." (Matthew 5: 43-44).

Did you read carefully Romans 12:17-19 cited earlier? On the heels of reminding us that revenge is up to God, not us, Paul tells us what our responsibility actually is. "Therefore if thine enemy hunger, feed him; if he thirst, give him drink; for in so doing thou shalt heap coals of fire on his head. Be not overcome of evil, but overcome evil with good." (Romans 12:20-21).

Forgiveness displayed virtually always must precede forgiveness felt. There is awesome power in acting out forgiveness. It can often melt even the hardest heart. If you are a minister, try these further suggestions.

Pay a friendly cordial visit to someone you have been ignoring, for no other motive than friendship. If you need to, and you are prompted by the Holy Spirit, ask forgiveness for your lack of demonstrated love.

The next time that committee meets which rejected your visionary idea, go with a smile on your face. Thank them for their desire to do the will of God. Invite their suggestions for how the church should be obedient to God.

Write an encouraging note to someone you know made an unkind remark about you. Make no mention of the offense.

Spend a half hour in prayer for that person whose attitude is obnoxious, and another for your own attitude. Get up and write them a note about some accomplishment or recognition they have recently received in the business world.

When you see that stubborn board member on Sunday, exchange pleasantries. Tell them a good joke and laugh with them.

Buy a sleeve of golf balls or a fishing lure for the man who snubbed you.

You will think of many more positive responses if you will allow yourself.

Churches Really Can Help

The pastor's congregation can help. I would never suggest that churches protect their ministers from resentment by accepting anything and everything carte blanche. Though I believe, completely, that pastors are to be the God-given, earthly leaders of the church, they can be wrong. *I would* suggest that people can seek to develop a close, personal relationship with the pastor. Let the pastor know he is accepted and loved.

Security grows from trust, and trust breeds greater security. Secure pastors rarely are dominated by resentment. Secure pastors trust their people. Pastors are not loved by a *congregation*. They are loved by the individuals that comprise that congregation. Give to the pastor the gift of being valued. Then, even if a particular idea of his is rejected, he will know that he, himself, is not rejected.

The willingness to forgive gives a refreshing charm to a person, a quality sadly missing in today's hostile world. Those who seem to thrive on anger and resentment become hardened and mark themselves as weak within. Surely that is a poor quality in the man of God. The person of forgiveness comes across as soft within, but by no means weak.

Someone unknown to me once wrote, "To forgive is to set a prisoner free, and then realize that the prisoner was me." Don't be a prisoner any longer. Don't destroy your joy by holding onto resentment. By the grace of God, learn to forgive as Jesus Christ has forgiven you. Your ministry will take on a new authenticity and power.

Chapter Three

The Unspoken Frustration of the Ministry: Comparison

L ike many advances of modern science and technology, television can be seen as a blessing or a curse. It is a source of information. Yet it has imprinted violence and sexual deviance upon children's minds. It brings us news of our world, yet it has brought the blood of battlefields into our living rooms.

Church leaders often criticize television and its effect on the moral state of the nation. However, we must be honest. Television has also helped us in our mission. As the year 2000 approached, many evangelical Christian groups established the goal of giving the whole world the best opportunity possible to hear and respond to the good news of Jesus Christ. Television was an obvious way to help fulfill that goal. Many saw this as one of the God-given ways to bring about the fulfillment of Jesus' prophecy, "And this gospel of the kingdom shall be preached in all the world for a witness unto all the nations, , and then shall the end come." (Matthew 24:14)

Some local churches have used television to great advantage in carrying out their own ministries. In many churches, shut-in members, or those who are ill on a particular Sunday, can still feel connected to their church family by watching the services on television.

It can hardly be denied, however, that some people use the availability of television ministries as an excuse for their lack of involvement in a local church, even when they are physically able. More frequently than ever, we hear people speak of "my TV pastor."

Many have noticed an even more subtle negative effect of television ministries on the local church and local church ministers. Not all pastors are delighted to know their parishioners are regularly dining at the spiritual tables with TV preachers. It is not that these local pastors are all paranoid or trying to cope with inferiority feelings. There is the very real issue of comparisons made between the highly visible and popular preachers on television, and the largely unknown and unrecognizable local parish pastor. The reminders come frequently. Church members may express the desire that the local pastor be or perform more like the media pastor.

In an earlier chapter, there was a brief discussion of how feelings of loneliness can be created when one has to bear continued questions about why he is not more like someone seen on television. Comparisons are probably inevitable. However, when these comparisons are continual, and when faithful pastors are made to feel inadequate, frustration rises.

Media ministers are presumed successful simply because they are able to broadcast. If they also have books and tapes available, speaking engagements across the country, ministries to the hungry and needy, these can all combine to give the appearance of great success. Ministries that are smaller, by comparison, may seem, and feel, unsuccessful. The truth is, of course, not all preachers on television have large churches, or "empires." Not all are as "successful" as those who are seen around the world.

Some of the preachers who appear weekly on television are articulate and polished. Otherwise, their audiences would not stay with them. By comparison, the pastor who occasionally uses incorrect grammar or cannot afford expensive suits seems unprofessional.

Many TV preachers are held to be the standard of excellence and correctness in interpreting and teaching the Bible. By contrast, the pastor who is faithful to his responsibilities but not nearly so eloquent seems backward. Some people would never think of questioning an interpretation of the Bible they hear from their hero on television. But they may reject the interpretation of the one who stands before them each week, in person.

During the confused days leading up to the turn of the calendar to the year 2000, some TV teachers and evangelists frightened a great many people with dire predictions. One pastor was approached by a single mother, a member of his church. She had heard on a broadcast ministry that people, especially single women, should buy firearms and large supplies of food and water. She questioned him as to his feelings about whether the "Y2K crisis" was the fulfillment of certain predictions in the book of *Revelation.* She wanted to know if he agreed with the evangelist she had heard (and had begun to support financially).

When the pastor urged calm and advised her that the incoming year would likely not be as cataclysmic as she feared, she pulled a huge sheaf of material from her briefcase and parroted the same case she had heard on television. "I can't be too careful," she said, "being a single mother, and all." She made no attempt to hide her disappointment at his disagreement with her TV pastor. Later, she confided to several people that her minister "was not very spiritual, and didn't believe the book of Revelation." She even left the church over the issue. It later became obvious who was correct, but no apologies were offered.

Most Christian leaders on television are undoubtedly people of honor. Few of them would encourage such comparisons. But they do occur. And the local church pastor often seems unsophisticated and less capable in the eyes of the public. Sometimes, those feelings are internalized by the pastor himself. Then, problems can result.

The standard of comparison is not always the television preacher, however. Church members generally remember their current pastor's predecessors with fondness and devotion. This is understandable if a particular minister had a long tenure. Perhaps he walked with a certain person through deep waters, or was present at a major spiritual or physical transition in their lives. The emotional ties forged by shepherding a person through conversion, the death of a loved one, victory over an addiction, and other important events are close. Of course, that person will tend to see that minister as the epitome of caring and strength. Words spoken in such times become virtually etched on their hearts.

Feelings can become inflated and abilities exaggerated over time, however. "He was a caring person," the parishioner may say; "He was the most caring minister I have ever known." No one who follows that minister will have much of a chance to measure up, at least for a long time.

What is amazing is that people often have a long memory for a predecessor's strengths, and a short memory for his weaknesses. The predecessor amazingly seems to have been gifted in the areas in which the present pastor is weak. Especially if you are a pastor following someone with a long tenure, be prepared for comparisons. It may seem like a long time before you are accepted as the "real pastor."

When a man I know had been in a particular church for ten years, he still occasionally heard people refer to him as the "new pastor." He had followed a man who was highly successful, well loved, and had stayed for fourteen years. So this friend grew to expect scrutiny.

If that has happened to you, instead of developing a spirit of resentment, seek to be grateful for the heritage that has been left for you. Without abandoning your own strengths and gifts, use this situation as an opportunity for personal growth.

Pastors are, however, not immune to the feelings of inadequacy and hurt brought about by such comparisons. Most people do not intend to be so blatant in their comparisons. Certainly, they do not intend to hurt their minister's feelings, but the hurt is often there, nonetheless.

Sometimes, the comparison is done by the pastor himself. Self-image problems do exist in the heart of many ministers. Pastors may base their feelings of success on statistical comparisons or on denominational recognition. I must admit I can remember telling my wife that although I enjoy attending my denomination's annual meeting, I often came away feeling inadequate after listening to sermons by certain homiletical heroes. I have engaged in comparison.

Comparisons are generally made based on external characteristics alone. It is easy enough to compare preaching styles, vocabulary, appearance, or vocal quality. And, of course, some are more gifted than others. But who says they are the standard by which all should be measured? It is not possible to measure a pastor's heart for God or his devotion to his people by any external standard. In that regard, one minister may have fewer physical marks of success than someone else, but an even greater faithfulness to the Lord. People do an injustice to that pastor, and he does an injustice to himself by measuring success based on externals.

The very fact that some ministers who had the marks of success, Hollywood looks, large churches, and name recognition have washed out of the ministry because of moral failure, proves that the externals are not supremely important. The minister with an ordinary or even homely appearance who faithfully endures in the service of God, loves people, and remains pure is a success in God's eyes even if not in his own.

There are many ways a minister may respond when, by comparison, he feels inadequate. He may **adopt certain physical styles** of one he considers to be *the standard*. Hair and clothing styles are easy ways to feel equal to someone admired. It is not usual at denominational meetings or conferences to see a well-known minister being followed by a group of ministers, usually younger, with similar hairstyles and suits.

One may study a hero in minute detail, and begin to adopt a notable characteristic of that hero. It might even be a negative one like a twitch, a speech defect, or a certain repeated phase for which the person has become known. It might be imitating a speech pattern or style of speaking. That could even involve affecting an accent, which usually produces humorous and embarrassing results.

During my seminary days, more than a few young preachers wanted to be like Billy Graham. The motive was not entirely wrong. Who could fault anyone wanting to be used by God as was Mr. Graham? A friend of mine at school was a youth evangelist, preaching revivals most weekends. When we saw each other, we usually extended a greeting, "I'm going to say good morning to you," in a typical Billy Graham style. My wife, Dianne, used to warn me to stop the imitation. "It *will* catch up to you one day," she predicted.

One weekend, I was invited to fill the pulpit at a church in Ft. Worth for the main Sunday morning service. Dianne accompanied me. When I was introduced, I went to the pulpit, and was shocked at what came out of my mouth, totally unplanned. I blurted out, "I'm going to ask that every head be bowed in prayer," a phrase I had heard Billy use a hundred times. I even affected his accent. I immediately glanced at Dianne who was sitting in the center section. She began giggling uncontrollably. I was rattled, and I completely forget everything I had planned to say. At least fifteen seconds went by before I could even lead the prayer. Because there were only about one hundred people present, at least I did not end up with "I'm going to ask hundreds of you to get up from your seats and come forward!"

Then I heard the Scottish brogue of a pastor in South Carolina. The lilt of his voice and the rolling of his "r's" sounded so much more spiritual and interesting than my flat Southern sounds. A friend made the comment, "A good accent is worth at least fifty more baptisms a year!" Fortunately, I did not attempt to copy that brogue, but I still felt that my speaking was boring.

There is always the temptation to structure one's sermons like a ministerial hero. Unquestionably, many young preachers do search for models as they are developing their own style. But, sometimes, they adopt some of the worst styles of others. Again, I learned some things the hard way.

When I was young in the ministry, I became enamored with a well-known expositor whose sermons are built around highly alliterative outlines. Call him Dr. Almond. This man has been a great spiritual influence on my life. However, I took his sermonic styles to an extreme. I knew it produced sermon outlines that were forced, but it seemed so much more profound than my simplistic style.

Later, there were other models, including a well-known Southern Baptist preacher known for his rapid-fire style. Call him Dr. Adams. My brother, who is a marvelous communicator of the Gospel, once asked me, in those early and formative years, what I thought my "style" was. I answered, "I think I am a combination between Dr. Almond and Dr. Adams."

I will never forget the look of incredulity on his face, nor how foolish I felt about my answer. I knew my alliterations made my messages hard to follow. I also know that my own speaking style was (and still is) rather slow. To speak with a machine-gun delivery was completely unnatural. Yet, I so wanted to be "effective" that I imitated my heroes, never thinking that it only made me *less* effective.

The desire to be a good communicator is commendable. However, adopting an unnatural style because of feelings of inadequacy born of comparison is not commendable.

An especially dangerous response is to literally preach the sermons of one who has become a hero. With easy access to printed or audio sermons on the Internet, some preachers fall into the habit of depending on the study and discipline of others when they go to their own pulpits. In most cases, no attempt is made to acknowledge the source of the sermon. Not only does such stealing (and it is stealing!) foster laziness in the pastor, messages crafted by someone else may not truly feed his own congregation. They do not grow out of his *own* walk with those God has given to *him* to shepherd. Because they are not the fruit of his own study and discipline, such messages often do not "ring true."

A further danger should be obvious, and that is exposure. Several years ago, a presidential candidate was forced out of the race for his party's nomination by revelations of plagiarism. Periodically, reports surface of ministers who are discovered parroting the words of others without giving credit. Of course, the embarrassment is great. Some justify such practices by the pressures of time and schedule, which we all experience. Some laugh it off with comments like the oft heard, "When better sermons are written, I'll preach them." Sometimes, however, the issue is simply that a minister believes that nothing he can prepare and deliver on his own could be as insightful, informative, or inspiring as sermons from one of the so called "sermonic champions." Again, the problem is comparison.

Comparison done by a congregation may show a lack of appreciation for a pastor's own strengths. It may even border on being cruel and manipulative. Comparison done by the minister himself may be seen as a sign of inadequate trust in God. God made each minister unique. Comparison assumes that a standard other than God's own design is the standard of effectiveness or success. In either case, it may be sinful.

The Apostle Paul gave wise words of counsel about this very issue in 2 Corinthians 10:12, "For we dare not make ourselves of the number, or compare ourselves with some that commend themselves: but they measuring themselves by themselves, and comparing themselves among themselves are not wise."

This is one of many Scripture passages which I understand in principle, but struggle to apply and practice. Read in context, Paul's statement grows out of several criticisms leveled at him. Christians in Corinth may have mocked him for his appearance. An ancient work described Paul as being short, with a large nose, and a face covered with unsightly warts. Perhaps this criticism was true.

He was apparently criticized for not being articulate because he did not use great rhetoric or philosophical arguments in his preaching as some other speakers did. Some may even have said that he did not speak with great authority. Perhaps, they even reminded him of his past as a persecutor of believers. In other places, Paul addressed each of those charges.

As to his not being *articulate*, or not using flowery language, he said,

"But we preach Christ crucified, unto the Jews a stumbling block, and unto the Greeks, foolishness; but unto them which are called, both Jews and Greeks, Christ the power of God, and the wisdom. Because the foolishness of God is wiser than men; and the weakness of God is stronger than men." (1 Corinthians 1:23-25)

"And I, brethren, when I came unto you, came not with excellency of speech or of wisdom, declaring unto you the testimony of God. For I determined not to know anything among you, save Jesus Christ and him crucified. And I was with you in weakness and in fear, and in much trembling. And my speech and my preaching was not with enticing words of man's wisdom, but in demonstration of the Spirit and of power. That your faith should not stand in the wisdom of men, but in the power of God." (1 Corinthians 2:1-5)

As to whether he spoke with *authority,* he reminded them of his status.

"Am I not an apostle? Am I not free? Have I not seen Jesus Christ our Lord? Are not ye my work in the Lord? If I be not an apostle unto others, yet doubtless I am unto you: for the seal of mine apostleship are ye in the Lord." (1 Corinthians 9:1-2)

In other words, he had the authority but did not beat them over the head with it.

Actually, he said he had more authority than some of the teachers with whom they were comparing him, for he was the first to bring them the good news of Christ.

"For though I should boast somewhat more of our authority, which the Lord hath given us for edification, and not for your destruction, if I should not be ashamed: that I may not seem as if I would terrify you by letters. For his letters, say they, are weighty and powerful, but his bodily presence is weak, and his speech contemptible. Let such a one think this, that such as we are in word by letters, when we are absent, such will we be also in deed when we are present." (2 Corinthians 10: 8-11)

"But we will not boast of things without our measure, but according to the measure of the rule which God hath distributed to us, a measure to reach even unto you. For we stretch not ourselves beyond our measure, as though we reached not unto you: for we are come as far as to you also in preaching the gospel of Christ." (2 Corinthians 10:13-14)

As to his past, he *acknowledged* it. However, he maintained that he had been totally forgiven

"And I thank Christ Jesus our Lord, who hath enabled me, for that he counted me faithful, putting me into the ministry, who was before a blasphemer, and a persecutor, and injurious, but I obtained mercy, because I did it in unbelief. And the grace of our Lord was exceeding abundant with faith and love which is in Christ Jesus. This is a faithful saying; and worthy of all acceptation, that Christ Jesus came into the world to save sinners; of whom I am chief. Howbeit it for this cause I obtained mercy, that in me first Jesus Christ might show forth all long-suffering, for a pattern to them which should hereafter believe on him to life everlasting. Now unto the King eternal, immortal, invisible, the only wise God, be honor and glory for ever and ever. Amen."
(1 Timothy 1:12-17)

Clearly, these people were basing their assessments of Paul on comparison with others who they considered to be more personally appealing or righteous. But Paul established the principle that our service to God and our gifts from God stand on their own. Thank the Lord we do not have to answer for what anyone else is or does. We are only responsible for what we do with what God has given us.

Some people are surprised to learn that the Bible even addresses the issue of comparison. The Divine Author did so because he knew how comparison tears at the fabric of biblical self-acceptance and creates negative emotions.

One application of this text has been to warn us of the danger of comparing ourselves, morally and spiritually, to others, to justify an unsaved condition. How many Christians, attempting to share their faith, have heard the objection, "He claims to be a Christian, but his life doesn't show it. Why should I need to be saved? I'm just as good as those Christians at your church."

I once heard Dr. Adrian Rogers say, "I'm waiting for someone to say, 'I'm just as bad as those Christians at your church.' The truth is, the church is the only organization other than the Hell's Angels you have to admit to be bad in order to join." All of us can find someone who makes us look bad or good. We can, by comparison, hide behind someone else to avoid seeing our own need of salvation. So the Lord gives us the principle, "Stop comparing. Face yourself and your own need." The only standard is the perfection of Christ and we all fall short of his glory, (Romans 3:23).

The argument has been made that this passage applies only to individuals comparing themselves to others. It should not, according to that position, but made to apply to others trying to force us into the mold of another. However, the fact that Paul wrote this sentence to those who were comparing him to other teachers belies that.

Paul was being deliberately general. He did not limit himself to moral or spiritual comparisons. The principle behind not comparing ourselves to others runs deep. It goes to the heart of God's thoughtful and perfect design of you. He deliberately did not make you walk, talk, or look like Billy Graham or anyone else. Recall here 2 Corinthians 10:12, "For we dare not make ourselves of the number, or compare ourselves with some that commend themselves: but they measuring themselves by themselves, and comparing themselves among themselves, are not wise."

That verse should be read side by side with Psalm 139:13-16, "For thou hast possessed my reins, thou hast covered me in my mother's womb. I will praise thee; for I am fearfully and wonderfully made; marvelous are thy works; and that my soul knoweth right well. My substance was not hid from thee when I was made in secret, and curiously wrought in the lowest parts of the earth. Thine eyes did see my substance, yet being unperfect, and in thy book all my members were written, which in continuance were fashioned, when as yet there was none of them."

Let every minister reading these words lay hold of several bedrock truths about his life and ministry, based on these passages.

God has uniquely gifted and equipped you for his service. To belittle or question your own abilities to serve God is, ultimately, to question God's sovereignty. To attempt to imitate someone else is actually to cover up the unique testimony God has given you. What you do with your gifts, *and limitations*, gives you a special witness no one else can duplicate.

God does not require that you be successful as the world, or your denomination, or other ministers may measure success. He only requires you to be faithful. Actually, faithfulness equals success in the Lord's eyes.

God made no mistake in designing you. If you do not accept that, there can be consequences in your spiritual life. More than one person who has been disgusted or unsatisfied with the things about him, which cannot be changed, has begun to doubt his salvation. Our hearts tell us consciously, "If God could not be trusted to make me better than this physically, he cannot be trusted spiritually either."

There will be no peace in your life if you struggle to "find yourself" by imitating others. If you serve a congregation that expects you to be everything their former pastor was, and you try to oblige them, you will be less than you are, in your uniqueness. And you may ruin yourself physically. Dr. J. Harold Smith once quipped, "Every preacher who trims himself to suit everybody will soon whittle himself away." There comes a time to accept who *you* are, develop your *own* style, be comfortable with *your* gifts, and leave the results to the Heavenly Father.

The last time I checked, God has no one human ideal for the pastor, not in style, not in appearance. The only model we are asked to follow is Jesus Christ, the great Shepherd. After that, there is a lot of room for variety. There is a place for those who wear tailored suits, or flannel shirts and jeans. There is room for those with melodic, resonant voices and those with hoarse whispers. The issue continues to be, are *you* faithful with *your* gifts?

47

If you struggle with a low self-image, if you feel woefully unsuccessful, is it perhaps because of comparison with others? You may need time alone with God, thanking him for *your* uniqueness. If you have built an image for yourself based on someone else's style or appearance, you may literally be *preventing* the effectiveness God wants you to have. Loosen up! Be more natural! You may be surprised at how people respond when they see the real you shining through. The real you are not as boring or inadequate as you think, because God designed you, and, as a little boy said, "God don't make no junk."

If you happen to follow a minister who stayed a long time in that position, and you feel you suffer by comparison, learn to be patient. It may not be fair, but you should not expect people to simply ignore the years he invested, any more that you would want them to ignore your service. That he is loved does not mean that you are unloved, unappreciated, or inadequate.

I once had a staff member who followed a much-loved person in his position. His attitude was perfect. He often said, "I am not threatened by the love and the relationship they had for him. It just gives me a glimpse of the love and relationship I could have with them." That kind of attitude made his a long-term stay, even though the two men were very different. My counsel? Plan to stay awhile in your present position of ministry and give your best. One day, you may be the standard by which the next person is measured. That may not be fair to him either, but it will probably like "poetic justice" to you.

Be yourself even though you consider your own style inadequate. You may learn, at first, by copying someone else. Move beyond that, in time.

Many years ago, at a Southern Baptist Pastor's Conference, I heard Dr. John Bisagno, then pastor of the First Baptist Church of Houston, Texas, preach. He was one of my heroes as a young pastor. He always "rang the bell" in the pulpit. He was always fresh and insightful. Fortunately, his style was inimitable!

He read 1 Corinthians 1:27-29 as his text, which says, "But God hath chosen the foolish things of the world to confound the wise; and God hath chosen the weak things of the world to confound the things that are mighty; and base things of the world; and things which are despised hath God chosen, yea and things which are not, to bring to nought things that are: that no flesh should glory in his presence."

He recounted his own attempts to find a "style" as a preacher. He thought he had found it at first by imitating others he considered, by comparison, to be more capable or successful than he was. He even did his impressions of great preachers like W.A. Criswell, Angel Martinez, J. Harold Smith, R. G. Lee, Hyman Appleman, and Billy Graham, and admitted to having copied them. The audience at the convention loved it.

His concluding words have been burned onto my heart. He said "You be you, known or unknown to this world. Be sweet you, be available you, be Spirit-filled you. Because as long as God chooses to use the weak things and the foolish things of this world, then cheer up, brother, there is hope for us all."

I am still struggling to live out the truth of that counsel, but I know it is biblical. I know it will ultimately make me more fulfilled and more effective in ministry, not less.

When David, the shepherd boy, was anointed by the prophet Samuel as the next king of Israel, he did not ascend to the throne immediately. He did, however, volunteer to fight Goliath. David's predecessor, King Saul, urged him to wear the king's own armor battle. After trying on the pieces of armor, he refused, saying, "I cannot go with these, for I have not proved them." (1 Samuel 17:39). And he took them off. (1 Samuel 17:39)

So how did David go to meet the giant? With what *he* knew best, the things *he* knew how to use.

"And he took his staff in his hand, and chose him five smooth stones out of the brook, and put them in a shepherd's bag which he had, even in a scrip, and his sling was in his hand: and he drew near to the Philistine." (1 Samuel 17:40)

All of us know the result. David was an instrument of God's power in victory.

Do not succumb to the temptation to approach your ministry with only a borrowed style. You won't be nearly so comfortable, and God will not receive the glory.

Allow me to share one further word of counsel. One of the most dangerous forms of comparison is comparing ourselves to other ministers who have fallen and lost their ministries. There is always the temptation to look at their tragedy and think smugly, "I would never do what they did." Some comparisons put us in danger of depression or feelings of inadequacy. The result may be imitation. This kind of comparison puts us in danger of pride and the result may be a fall in our own lives. It is no accident that Paul wrote in Galatians 6:1-5, "Brethren, if a man be overtaken in a fault, ye which are spiritual, restore such a one in the spirit of meekness, considering thyself, lest thou also be tempted. Bear ye one another's burdens, and so fulfill the law of Christ. For if a man think himself to be something when he is nothing, he deceiveth himself. But let every man prove his own work, and then he shall have rejoicing in himself alone, and not in another. For every man shall bear his own burden."

The Church Can Take the Pressure off the Pastor

It is important that a few words be said to lay persons reading this chapter.

By all means, love your former pastor or staff member, but don't impose expectations and roles based on comparisons on the one who currently fills that position. Kindness should reign in your new relationship. Expectations based on comparison are rarely fair. To force the pastor to be something other than who God gifted him to be puts unnecessary pressure on him. You will not receive the blessing that God wants you to have of a pastor serving in freedom. He probably really is seeking to follow God's lead and give you God's best. He may show nothing but graciousness in his manner but he is likely chafing and hurting at the unfair expectations. Granting him freedom is the best way to have an effective minister.

Remember the limitations of a TV pastor separated from you by circuit boards and satellite dishes and many miles, as compared to the faithful servant God has put in your midst. The one you watch on television will never come to your bedside in the hospital or counsel you when your marriage is in trouble, but your pastor will. The one on the screen simply can't equal the one on the scene.

The TV evangelist may be a prince of preachers but he can't preach like a pastor. Your pastor, if he is doing his job (as most do), will know you, pray for you, and address your real needs because he has walked with you. He will give you warmth that even a High Definition picture cannot transmit. Appreciate him for who he is. Yes, he has weaknesses. But there are also things he can do that no one else can. Magnify and be grateful for *those* things.

And recognize this if you are using televised services as a substitute for involvement in a local church. At least one reason people may retreat to an impersonal TV church family is that it makes no real demands. Turning on a switch doesn't require much dedication. Sending in a monthly gift or even tossing the request letter into the wastebasket is easier than facing up to the responsibilities of being part of a visible church.

Help your church come to a clear understanding of what the major focus of a pastor's ministry will be, *before* he assumes the position. Then, stay with that commitment, unless you and he both agree a new direction is needed. If the former pastor was a wonderful administrator and you want your new pastor to mainly work at "oiling wheels," fine. But choose an administrator for that position. Don't call a pastor whose gifts are obviously in pulpit ministry and force him to neglect or abandon that gift to be something he is not. No one will be fulfilled or blessed.

That is not to say ministers cannot and should not grow in their ministries. Maturing ministers will grow. But it should be because of personal convictions given by God, not because expectations birthed through comparison.

On the dedication page of this book, I expressed gratitude and appreciation for my brother. I could have also dedicated it to the church I serve, as of this writing. They have given me the freedom to be who I am. In our earliest conversations together about my becoming their pastor, we reflected together on my gifts. I am gifted in teaching, preaching, and, to some degree, writing. I am a communicator. I do other things related to ministry because they are part of my ministry. I am competent in them, but I am best at communication. The church and I are both most fulfilled when I focus primarily on my main gifts. They wanted someone whose major emphasis was the preaching and teaching ministry. They chose me, knowing who *I* was.

I take my other responsibilities seriously and work hard at them. About 1989, I realized the need to grow in other areas, including relationships. I began to focus more there, without neglecting my preaching responsibilities. The response was interesting. I was even more fulfilled, and so were they. My preaching took on more of a personal tone than an academic tone. I was not just a pastor who had to preach. I was not just a preacher who had to pastor. I became a preaching pastor.

The point is, I am grateful for the freedom. My predecessor was very much a people person and an excellent administrator. He stayed a long time. He and I are good friends. There were, for several years, some comparisons. But for the most part, this church allows me, and other staff members, to be ourselves. I have now outstayed my predecessor by many years. I have no illusions that I am the new standard for ministry here. But as we have grown older together, pastor and people are becoming more like a matched set. We blend well. We are both more fulfilled because of the removal of the pressure caused by comparison.

Chapter Four

The Unspoken Hypocrisy of the Ministry: Prayerlessness

I t has happened to everyone, not just ministers. A friend says, "Please pray for me," then describes a need which sounds desperate. The first reaction is to say, "Of course, I will." The conversation ends with those familiar words, "I'll be praying for you." At the moment we say them, we have every intention of honoring that promise. Perhaps, on occasion we hear a need, we think to ourselves, "That doesn't sound terribly serious," and cut off discussion with what amounts to a cliché, "I'll be praying about that." All the while, we know we probably won't.

Most of the time, however, we realize the importance of the need, and understand our responsibility as a friend or as a pastor to pray. Unfortunately, we often forget you pray as we promised. All of us know the embarrassment of having that friend come up to us and say, "I could feel your prayers. I just knew you were lifting me up." We smile, and say, "I'm so glad it worked out," but never admit our forgetfulness. Inside, we repent of the negligence, and resolve to do better the next time. Yet the pattern repeats itself.

Broken promises to pray may be testimony to how busy we are, or to our forgetfulness. However, they also speak of our lack of discipline. Worse still, they often reveal the inner belief that prayer is not as effective as our own attempts to help in human strength. That often reveals inadequate trust in the power of God.

I remember an incident when I was in college. A friend asked me to pray about a situation in his family. As I recall, it was about a court hearing involving his father. I promised to pray at a given hour. My next memory of that promise was about six hours after the agreed-upon hour. I felt guilty about forgetting my promise.

I also remember crafting an extremely creative prayer upon remembering. I said something like, "Lord, I know time means nothing to you. In your eyes, eight o'clock tonight is no different than two o'clock this afternoon. You knew I meant to pray at two. You also knew I would forget and think about it only now. Receive my prayer now as a pray for my friend's family. Make it as though my prayer now, which is late, was a prayer before, which would have been just in time."

I know virtually nothing about Einstein's Theory of Relativity. But I had heard it had something to do with space and time, and that time has no meaning. Maybe I thought I could apply that to the spiritual realm and make up for forgetting my promise of timely prayer. Somehow, I doubt I am the only one who has tried such twisted means of getting around broken prayer promises.

The place the minister is most often confronted with requests is at the door of the worship center after a service. That is a time he is most accessible. Someone says, "My sister is having surgery on Tuesday at nine. Please pray for her." As we shake his or her hand, we promise, and then just as quickly forget. Members often do not recognize that at that moment, the minister has a thousand things on his mind. He is weary from the physical and emotional drain of preaching. If there has been little or no response to his message, he may feel discouraged. Prayer requests do not stick well to a memory already cluttered with such thoughts. He means well, but he forgets.

Occasionally, I see statistics about the amount of time professional clergy spend in prayer during the course of a week's responsibilities. The most recent survey I have seen reveals that the average senior pastor spends approximately seven minutes per week specifically in prayer. That does not reflect public prayers in worship services, prayer before meals, or prayer at various church functions.

That statistic is shocking and disappointing to those of us who are pastors, we almost want the information suppressed and hidden from our congregations. We simply do not want our people to know how little time we spend in prayer. We preach to them about praying. We know its importance in the ministry of the church. But, we ourselves often do not do it. Does that sound even remotely like hypocrisy? But who can we tell about the deficiencies in our personal spiritual lives, lest we be thought unspiritual, or even unworthy of the title, "pastor"?

What we don't recognize is that the more discerning and spiritually sensitive may already know it. Continuing neglect of prayer produces a minister whose heart is fertile ground for pride, a domineering spirit, anger, anxiety, or defensiveness. His reactions begin to show a person who is "on edge" because he has not spent time "casting all his cares on the Lord (1 Peter 5:7)."

In the minister's defense, rarely is it deliberate refusal to pray. Rarely is it a conscious doubt of the power of God which can be released in prayer.

Every minster I know believes in prayer. We preach on it, some more frequently than others. For several years, I received the sermon tapes of a friend serving a church in Alabama. I marveled at the frequency of his preaching on new dimensions of prayer he had discovered. That stimulated me to do the same. My private prayer life, however, did not keep pace.

We offer training seminars on prayer and show videos on prayer. We follow our denominational calendar with its special prayer emphases. We believe that prayer is a major discipline of every Christian's life. When Richard Foster's book, *Celebration of Discipline* (Harper/San Francisco) was published, I read it, with special attention to the section on prayer. I realized *my* personal prayer life needed a jump start.

We ministers know that prayer must be *a foundation of church life*. What else could account for the explosion of life in the early church except a commitment to the basics, including prayer?

"And they continued steadfastly in the apostles' doctrine and fellowship, and in breaking of bread, and in prayers.And fear came upon every soul: and many wonders and signs were done by the apostles. And all that believed were together, and had all things common. And sold their possessions and goods, and parted them to all men, as every man had need. And they, continuing daily and with one accord in the temple, and breaking bread from house to house, did eat their meat with gladness and singleness of heart, praising God, and having favor with all the people. And the Lord added to the church daily such as should be saved." (Acts 2:42-47)

Certainly, the Bible reveals that prayer is *part of the job description* for a minster, to say nothing of his *tie to divine power*. In the midst of a crisis in the Jerusalem church over neglect of certain widows, the apostles urged the selection of a new group of servant leaders to deal with that situation. The result would be that they (the apostles) could focus on other things. Note, they did not want to be freed *from* some things so much as they wanted to be freed *to* the things they were primarily called to do. The apostles revealed their understanding of the basics of ministry in their words.

"Then the twelve called the multitude of the disciples unto them and said, It is not reason that we should leave the word of God, and serve tables. Wherefore, brethren, look ye out among you seven men of honest report, full of the Holy Ghost and wisdom, whom we may appoint over this business. But we will give ourselves continually to prayer, and to the ministry of the word. " (Acts 6:2-4)

Prayer is clearly part of the ministry of those called to shepherd a flock. Yet it often receives minor status in our schedules.

Certainly, we understand the church cannot be successful without a foundation of prayer. We know many of the *admonitions* to pray in the Scriptures.

"Seek the Lord and his strength, seek his face continually." (1 Chronicles 16:11)

"Watch and pray, that ye enter not into temptation: the spirit indeed is willing, but the flesh is weak." (Matthew 26:41)

"Praying always with all prayer and supplication in the Spirit, and watching thereunto with all perseverance and supplication for all the saints." (Ephesians 6:18)

We know the promises God makes to those who give themselves faithfully to prayer.

"He shall call upon me and I shall answer him: I will be with him in trouble; I will deliver him, and honor him." (Psalm 91:15)

"And I say unto you, ask and it shall be given unto you; seek, and ye shall find; knock, and it shall be opened unto you." (Luke 11:9)

"If ye abide in me, and my words abide in you, ye shall ask what ye will, and it shall be done unto you." (John 15:7)

"If my people, which are called by my name, shall humble themselves and pray, and seek my face, and turn from their wicked ways; then will I hear from heaven, and will forgive their sin, and will heal their land." (2 Chronicles 7:14)

The list could go on and on.

We even know there are *personal and physical benefits* that result from prayer. A physician in my congregation regularly passes on to me articles in his medical journals noting the measurable benefits of prayer. Consistently, I see reports of lower blood pressure, lower incidence of heart disease, and generally better health among those who report prayer as a regular part of their lives.

We also know, or at least we should, the Bible's *warnings about not praying*. There is a spiritual dullness that comes upon one's life, especially in the form if insensitivity to conviction of sin and an inability to grasp spiritual truth. While they were prisoners in Babylon, Daniel recognized the dullness in the people of Israel and attributed it to a failure to call on God.

"As it is written in the law of Moses, all this evil is come upon us: yet made we not our prayer before the Lord our God, that we might turn from our iniquities, and understand the truth." (Daniel 9:13)

If your life seems to be one long string of disasters, is God seeking to command your undivided attention? Are you unable to recognize His hand in the storms because your heart is not seeking Him regularly in prayer? As I am writing these words, I have sought Him for a change of attitude about my trials and recommitted myself to a life of prayer. To write about the hypocrisy of prayerlessness yet not pray myself would be double hypocrisy on my part. I do not wish to live without, and I know I cannot minister without, spiritual power. But that will be the result if my heart is dull toward God. Perhaps, you should also make that same recommitment before reading the next paragraph.

There is a consequence of prayerlessness that should be a special concern to spiritual leaders, specifically, fruitlessness in ministry, and division among the people of God.

"For the pastors are become brutish, and have not sought the Lord: therefore they shall not prosper, and all their flocks shall be scattered." (Jeremiah 10:21)

What spiritual shepherd would want to deliberately invite such confusion in his own life and that of his flock? None of whom I know! Yet we do when we do not pray.

One of the most chilling consequences noted in the Word of God is from the book of *Job*.

"Therefore they say unto God, depart from us; for we desire not the knowledge of thy ways. What is the Almighty that we should serve him? And what profit should we have, if we pray unto him?

As long as we believe that prayer is primary for our benefit, when we pray and see no results, we will easily become frustrated. Frustration may lead to giving up on prayer all together. That will produce the ultimate enemy of ministry, spiritual deadness. Part of the answer, of course, is remembering that prayer is not to meet our needs. Prayer is to meet God, which is our greatest need.

The positive results of prayer on ministry are nowhere more obvious than in the book of Acts. The apostles had the power to preach their way into jail and the power to pray their way out again. Because of prayer, their lives and ministries were filled with boldness. There is no better example than the following:

"And when they had prayed, the place was shaken where they were assembled together; and they were all filled with the Holy Ghost." (Acts 4:31)

Doubtless, few of us have ever prayed so effectively that the walls shook. Perhaps, God doesn't work exactly like that any longer. But he certainly does still promise to give us holy boldness as we preach and witness. Prayerlessness, by contrast, produces timidity and a spirit of reluctance to speak boldly for the Lord.

Years ago, I added a quotation to my files from Pastor E. M. Bounds. It speaks to the crisis of prayerlessness and powerlessness in out ministries.

The pulpit of this day is weak in praying. The pride of learning is against the dependent humility of prayer. Prayer is with the pulpit too often only an official act, a performance for the routine of the worship services. Prayer is not to the modern pulpit the mighty force it was in Paul's life or Paul's ministry. Every preacher who does not make prayer a mighty factor in his own life and ministry is weak as a factor in God's work and is powerless to protect God's cause in this world" (E.M. Bounds, "Power Through Prayer," Chicago, IL., Moody Press, 1985, p. 27)

At this point, I feel the need to warn readers against simply taking the points above turning them into another sermon or teaching outline. What is most needed is that God's Word be allowed to speak a convicting word to us if necessary. Have we approached our ministries on the basis of our professional training instead of the basis of prayer? Do we feel so competent to handle crises that we launch right in without praying? Has reading books become more of a foundation for sermon preparation than prayer? Do we really seek to model a life of prayer before those to whom we minister?

I suppose I have never attended a conference on the life of a minister without hearing some reference to the minister's prayer life. That is as it should be. But those conferences often only increase the already nagging sense of guilt we feel about our lagging prayer life. How often have I heard the familiar quote from John Wesley, "I have so much to do that I must spend hours in prayer before I am able to do it."

All have been confronted with the challenge to "rise early for prayer" by some of the spiritual giants of the past. We have gone home and tried to get up at 4:00 P.M. to pray, only to go to sleep on our knees or in our prayer chair. Repeated failures like that have made some of us believe we cannot succeed as prayer warriors, so we give up.

Dr. Paul W. Powell, a past president of the Southern Baptist Convention's Annuity Board, gives a helpful perspective on this issue.

> If I had my ministry to do over, one thing I'd do is pray more. I never felt like my prayer life was adequate. I have read of the great saints of other generations who spent an hour or more in prayer every day. That used to bother me until I realized they lived and ministered before the telephone and the automobile and the pressures of the modern pastorate. I don't think I could have ever found that much time for prayer, but, nonetheless, I wish I had prayed more.

> To neglect prayer is to neglect the source of the greatest power in our lives. If we depend on education, we get what education can do. If we depend on organization, we get what organization can do. If we depend on promotion, we get what promotion can do. But if we depend on prayer, we get what God can do.

I'm convinced that prayer is the principle work of a minister, and it is by it that he carries on the rest. Prayer does not fit us for greater works; prayer is the greater work.

President's Newsletter
Annuity Board of the Southern Baptist
Convention, Dallas, 1995

Do not be under guilt about an hour or a place for prayer. Now, I do believe morning is the time most people would experience the most effectiveness in prayer. Certainly, a specific place reserved for prayer helps to focus our concentration. Guilt trips, however, do not produce hearts ready to pray. Allow the Lord to direct you to a time, a place, and most of all, a motivation to pray.

Resistance to Praying

Recently, I was discussing with a friend the idea for this chapter. Before entering the ministry, he was an attorney with a reputation as a hard-driving charger. Like the college football player he was, he seized life and ministry with both hands and tore into it. Since a marvelous encounter with the Holy Spirit, so much about him changed. He said, "Stewart, the main issue with which I struggle in regard to a prayer life is my Type A personality. I just have a hard time slowing down enough to pray."

If I recall correctly, what used to be called "Type A personality" is now called an obsessive-compulsive personality." I have often termed myself a Type AA personality. So I know the problem. One reason we resist praying is that prayer seems to slow an *approach to problems*. I want things done now! Many pastors, especially of larger churches, tend to have such personalities. Some are influenced by more CEO model of leadership than by the servant model. In that regard, manipulating circumstances and issuing orders to get things done seems far more efficient than spending time in prayer.

Bill Hybels, pastor of one of the largest churches in the United States, reveals another reason for prayerlessness.

Prayer has not always been my strong suit. For many years, even as senior pastor of a large church, I *knew* more about prayer than I ever *practiced* in my own life. I have a racehorse temperament. The tugs of self-sufficiency are very real to me. I didn't want to get off the fast track long enough to find out what prayer is all about ("Too Busy Not to Pray," Inter Varsity Press, Downers Grove, Illinois, 1988, p.9).

Lets' admit it, *prayer is an unnatural activity.* We have been fed the line that the mark of maturity is to achieve self-sufficiency. We have been taught we have all the resources we need within ourselves. Ministers fall prey to that belief. It fits very naturally with our old sin nature that seeks independence from the Lord. Prayer is an affront to our pride. To people driving in the fast lane, prayer can seem more like a slow moving Model T that won't get out of our way.

Some ministers rationalize that *praying as they study and prepare to teach is enough.* Few ministers would fail to pray as they prepare to preach and teach. We know that spiritual things are spiritually discerned and that the Holy Spirit must be our teacher (1 Corinthians 2:9-15).

So we pray over Scripture. The presumption that this is sufficient to cover, enrich, and empower all of our ministries, however, is a deception.

Sometimes, honestly, it seems easier to address a situation in preaching than pray about it. It seems to produce faster results. How many sermons about problem issues or problem people have been for the purpose of manipulating a circumstance immediately, rather than taking it before the Heavenly Father?

Others of us seem determined to *worry about a situation* instead of praying about it. We ministers know well Paul's admonition,

"Be careful for noting; but in every thing by prayer and supplication with thanksgiving let your requests be made known unto God. And the peace of God which passeth all understanding shall keep your hearts and minds through Christ Jesus." (Philippians 4:6-7)

Yet, we seem to prefer stewing in our own juices, or letting our minds run around in circles wearing holes in themselves, rather than giving the circumstance over to God in prayer. How many of our anxieties and frustrations have we taken out on our people from the pulpit because we did not take the time to gain heart peace in our place of prayer?

Prayerlessness is a trap. It begins for a variety of reasons. The longer we remain virtually prayerless, depending on our skills or our work ethic to accomplish our ministry, the harder it is to break out of the trap. If we preach and teach on prayer but don't practice it, we feel the twinge of hypocrisy. If it remains something we do not confess and talk about, we will descend further into powerlessness, fruitlessness, and perhaps even deadness.

In kindness, I should repeat, however, that the majority of the time the problem is *forgetfulness*. We intend to be people of prayer. We intend to honor the requests for prayer. We intend to master our busy schedules and build in time to seek God's hand and God's face. We know it is sinful to tell others to pray yet not pray ourselves. But we forget.

The prophet Samuel addressed the issue of prayerlessness in his life and ministry in unqualified terms.

"Now therefore behold the king whom ye have chosen, and whom ye have desired! And behold the Lord hath set a king over you. If ye will fear the Lord, and serve him and obey his voice, and not rebel against the commandment of the Lord, then shall both ye and also the king that reigneth over you

continue following the Lord your God: but if ye will not obey the voice of the Lord, but rebel against the commandment of the Lord, then shall the hand of the Lord be against you, as it was against your fathers. Now therefore stand and see this great thing, which the Lord will do before your eyes. Is it not wheat harvest today? I will call upon the Lord, and he shall send thunder and rain; that ye may perceive and see that your wickedness is great, which ye have done in the sight of the Lord, in asking for a king. So Samuel called unto the Lord; and the Lord sent thunder and rain that day: and all the people greatly feared the Lord and Samuel. And all the people said unto Samuel, pray for thy servants unto the Lord thy God, that we die not: for we have added unto all our sins this evil, to ask us a king. And Samuel said unto the people, fear not: ye have done all this wickedness: yet turn not aside from following the Lord, but serve the Lord with all your heart; and turn ye not aside: for then should ye go after vain things, which cannot profit nor deliver; for they are vain. For the Lord will not forsake his people for his great name's sake, because it hath pleased the Lord to make you his people. Moreover, as for me, God forbid that I should sin against the Lord in ceasing to pray for you: but I will teach you the good and right way. Only fear the Lord, and serve Him in truth with all your heart: for consider how great things he hath done for you. But if ye shall still do wickedly, ye shall be consumed, both ye and your king."
(2 Samuel 12:13-25)

These verses must be put in context. The prophetic ministry of Samuel on behalf of God to the nation of Israel was coming to a close. The above words are part of his "farewell speech" delivered at a sacred site called Gilgal.

Samuel, as part of his responsibilities as a prophet, confronted the people with their sins against God. Some of those sins were idolatry, rebellion, and ingratitude. He reminded them of God's work in their history. Samuel had boldly rebuked their sins before, always stressing that God would forgive them if they repented. Yet, instead of repenting, they had demanded to have a king ruling over them, as did other nations. Throughout her history, Israel had trusted in God alone to rule over the nation and speak his will through the prophets and priests. Now they seemed to feel that human problems had primarily human solutions.

Through Samuel warned them against this different course, the people persisted, so Samuel had been instructed by God to choose a king. Saul became the first human king over Israel. Again, Samuel speaks the clear word that this new trust in a human ruler was sin against God. The problem, however, was not so much the desire for a king itself. The sin of Israel was that the people were substituting human solutions for divine solutions. They wanted the benefits of a relationship with God and stability in their national life without the demand of repentance. Samuel, with the insight of a prophet, recognized the signs of spiritual drift, pride, and self-reliance in the people.

Samuel called for a physical manifestation of God's awesome power and his displeasure with the people's sin. It came as a violent thunderstorm. The people, recognizing God's presence, cried out in confession. Samuel once again assured them of God's forgiveness.

Samuel had asserted his own spiritual authority. He had exercised the prophetic side of his ministry. Then, he acknowledged the responsibility to pray for them, in spite of their stubbornness and slow response.

Like Samuel, pastors deal with some people who are spiritually dull, ungrateful, and unresponsive. Yet, we are to pray for them. Samuel had failed to pray for the people of God. Samuel knew he would not have sinned just against them, but against God. Prayer is a duty toward God. Prayerlessness leaves us without God's power. Prayerlessness results in a ministry only half-done.

A Recommitment to Prayer

It would be easy enough to add to the pastor's load of guilt by borrowing the popular advertising phrase and admonish him to simply, "Do it." A part of me functions almost totally on the motivation of responsibility and self-discipline. I have been known to feel impatient with those who are *not* as disciplined. However, I feel the need in this chapter to do more than simply issue declarations and exhortations. As important as the discipline of prayer may be, there are other ways to develop an inward motivation to minister through prayer.

Begin by *saturating your life with the Scriptural admonitions to pray.* My life was changed by several summers working at a Christian sports camp and retreat center in the mountains of South Carolina. Its name, Look-Up Lodge, was drawn from Psalm 5:3 which reads,

My voice shalt thou hear in the morning, O Lord; in the morning will I direct *my prayer* unto thee, and will look up.

It was there that I began the pattern of early rising for a time alone with God. There have been numerous times of failure to keep that regular appointment. Those were also the times of spiritual drought and fruitlessness in my life and ministry. I go back to that and other verses periodically to rekindle the flame of desire to "meet God in the morning."

We must always *recognize the need in us* for a life of prayer. How frequently we read of the prayer life of Jesus!

"And in the morning, rising up a great while before day, he went out, and departed into a solitary place, and there prayed." (Mark 1:35)

"And it came to pass in those days, that he went out into a mountain to pray, and continued all night in prayer to God." (Luke 6:12)

If even the Son of God needed to fortify Himself by prayer, and saw prayer as one of the foremost ways to minister to people, should we not also?

One of the best ways to spend more time in prayer is to *pray at seemingly odd moments* such as while driving or waiting in a line of traffic. The police might take a dim view of you closing your eyes at such times! The driver next to you might think you were a bit strange if you prayed verbally at such time! So, let it be your heart connecting with the Father's heart as the Holy Spirit prompts you. I believe I remember reading one writer who called this practice, "flash praying." This would certainly help in fulfilling the biblical command to

...pray without ceasing... 1 Thessalonians 5:17

It is clearly a way to fulfill yet another command to "redeem the time," because of the evil days in which we live (Ephesians 5:16).

If you still do things the old-fashioned way, perhaps you could carry 3"x5" cards in your automobile marked with specific requests to use at such times. Perhaps you could put your prayer requests on an electronic device and keep it handy as a reminder. Perhaps you could ask God for a heart so sensitive to need around you that you are stimulated to pray as you see people or neighborhoods. A popular method of spiritual warfare and intercession is called "prayer walking." We could all practice "prayer driving" as we drive to and from appointments. Has your church penetrated that new apartment complex or subdivision with a witness? Bathe that area and your opportunity in prayer whenever you pass it.

As a pastor in a college town, I am often fascinated by the sights of students and the way they dress. Piercings, tattoos, strange hair colors, and baggy pants are common in my city. I will admit that, at times, I have felt the extremes of amusement and disgust at things I have seen. Recently, however, when I drive in the areas where students are walking, I have sought to pray for them, though I do not know their names. When a student walks in front of me while I am stopped at a red light, I may pray, "Lord, the signs of rebellion, spiritual emptiness, and searching are so obvious in that young man. Please put someone into his life that has found the answer in you, someone to whom he will listen. May he see the answers and the source of real life to be found in you." Practiced frequently enough, that kind of prayer can become a meaningful habit.

Intersperse times of heart worship along with your requests in prayer. Perhaps you could include tapes or CDs of worshipful music while you pray. Continual petitions addressed to God may grow wearying, but the human heart that is right with God craves the opportunity to exalt and worship him. Again, this practice can be done either in a formal prayer setting or the spur of the moment opportunities to pray, prompted by the Spirit. You will grow to deeply desire such moments, rich with the sense of God's presence.

In fact, our whole perspective of prayer needs changing. It is not just asking things of God. Prayer is also the deliberate time exposure of the soul to God. Many have noted that prayer is seeking God's face, not just seeking His hand.

Prayer is more about deepening a relationship than getting an answer. Again, I have found Bill Hybel's words helpful.

The greatest fulfillment in my prayer life has not been the list of miraculous answers to prayers I have received, although that has been wonderful. The greatest thrill has been the qualitative difference in my relationship with God. And when I started to pray, I didn't know what was going to happen. God and I used to be rather casually related to one another. We didn't get together and talk very much. Now, however, we get together a lot—not talking on the run, but carrying on substantial, soul-searching conversations every morning for a good chunk of time. I feel as if I've gotten to know God a lot better since I started praying. (Op. cit, p 9-10)

Instead of thinking, "I have to pray," *change your perspective on prayer* to "I get to pray." Prayer is a glorious privilege. Prayer is time alone with our Creator, Savior, Sustainer, and Friend, in which we have His full and undivided attention!

When I began to grow roses as a hobby, I quickly realized they required a tremendous amount of attention and work. Someone counseled me, that instead of thinking, "I have to work in the rose garden today," I should think, "I get to go visit my roses today." I tried it, and it worked! The same approach may help with developing a regular prayer life. Think, "This morning I have the privilege of spending time with the One who loves me more than anyone, the One who satisfied my heart," and you will develop a love for that time.

Prayer is a means of making our hearts big enough to receive the revelation of God He wants to give us. Most of us desire a fuller knowledge of God. We expand our capacity to know Him as we pray.

In 1998, Yehudi Menuin, the famous concert violinist, announced he was taking a two-year leave of absence from the stage. When asked why, he reportedly said, "I am not tired of playing. I simply need some time for just me and my Stradivarius." We desperately need time for just deepening our intimacy with the Almighty, or the pressures of ministering will dominate our lives. Then, neither we, nor those we serve, will be fulfilled.

In addition, there are *certain strategies* to help us be more committed to and more effective in prayer. Because they are so familiar to most of us, I will not belabor them here. They deserve mention, however. A *specific time* for prayer should be settled. The choice of a *place reserved for prayer* in important. It may be a room, or even a corner of a room, but it should be a place with minimal possibility of distraction.

Using a method for keeping our prayers focused is helpful. Many Christians have learned the ACTS formula: Adoration, Confession, Thanksgiving, and Supplication. The order of the letters and the practice is not unimportant. Worship (adoration) and confession should precede petitions (supplication). Often, we virtually reverse the order to STAC (supplication, thanksgiving, adoration, confession). When we do so, we "stack" our time against God. Instead of enjoying our time with Him, we will come to find it a burden, and do less of it.

In light of the fact that some of us have become a bit hypocritical about praying, yet resist admitting our prayerlessness, I must add this admonition. Make yourself accountable to someone you trust concerning your prayer habits. As hard as it may be to acknowledge an inadequate personal prayer ministry, the sound barrier must be broken. Enlist someone who will regularly ask about your prayer time. It is far better to do that, than to have your life take on the characteristics of a prayerless life, anxiety, a lack of self-control, pride, and even spiritual dullness. Those qualities are exposed before everyone.

If the problem truly is forgetfulness, find ways to help you remember. One pastor I know always has either a secretary or one of the ushers by his side when he greets people at the doors of the church. When someone mentions a prayer request, his aide writes it down immediately. That request ends up on his desk with other ongoing prayer requests. You can find a system that fits your situation.

Every congregation wants a pastor and staff with the qualities of spiritual depth, patience, and confidence produced by a deep prayer life. Every congregation wants a preacher with the kind of insights into the Word of God that only result from a deep prayer life. Preaching informed only by commentaries and other reading is often passionless and mechanical. Preaching that is bathed in prayer takes on a quality that can only be described as the Word taking on flesh again. Many pastors are willing to spend the time required in prayer, but their daily responsibilities nip at their heels like frantic dogs.

The Church Can Help Facilitate Pastoral Prayer

The congregation that wants a praying pastor or staff must allow them to structure their own schedules so as to reserve adequate time for prayer. Periodically, I publish what I attempt as my daily schedule. With all my heart, I seek to reserve the morning hours for prayer and study. If I let those hours go for counseling, visitation or any of the hundreds of other things I could be doing, soon I will not have those hours for prayer. Every time I state the desire, I learn that someone has been offended that I am "not available" for them. The truth is, of course, I am often ministering specifically on their behalf before the throne of God.

Consider this a plea to church members to allow your pastoral staff the time to pray. The benefits to you may not appear as quickly as time spent face to face with them. A pastor who has been face to face with God, on the other hand, will ultimately be of more help to you by far. Receiving the benefits of a minister who prays, means however, that members must relinquish their perceived right to set his schedule for him. One of my staff is a man whose prayer life would be worth imitation by any of us. He reserves specific hours each week for prayer. The result is that though he is fairly young, he has great patience, wisdom, creativity, and courage, qualities that make for a most successful ministry.

Years ago, I heard Dr. Wayne Dehoney, then pastor of Walnut Street Baptist Church in Louisville, Kentucky, tell the following story. In the 1940's a Dr. Pettigrew was pastor of the church. One Sunday evening, the auditorium was cold during the evening service. While Dr. Pettigrew was preaching, a man went to the basement to check the furnace. The man came back upstairs, walked into the auditorium, and announced in a voice loud enough for many to hear, "The furnace is off, but the blower is still going!"

Many a preacher has been humbled by the realization that his ministry has reached the point that he is producing air, still going through the motions, but the heat of spiritual power is missing. Often, he discovers that a superficial prayer life is the cause. That is often enough motivation to drive him to pray.

When he discovers, however, that prayer *is* his ministry, and not only the supporter of his ministry, he has an even greater reason to pray. The realization that your ministry is devoid of prayer can produce feelings of humiliation. Let the embarrassment drive you into a deeper commitment to pray, rather than into simply paralyzed silence.

Chapter Five

The Unspoken Pain of the Ministry: Sadness

Two friends were drinking coffee together. They were sharing very personal things about their lives. One named Stephen acknowledged an ongoing struggle with feelings of anxiety and fear, which had led him into a valley of sadness. He feared it was becoming depression. He didn't like what he was feeling at all, because, basically, he considered himself to be an optimist in his outlook on life.

His friend Bradley, who was known for his sunny disposition, tried to cheer Stephen up. He said, "We all have our ups and downs." Stephen looked at his friend with a gaze that revealed his deep frustration and replied, "Why? Why must we have ups and downs? Why can't we just stay on a high?" Emotions, especially so-called "negative emotions," are trivial to some people. The expectations that one can or should have all "positive emotions" create not only disappointment and frustration, but also surprise when the "down times" come. The worst reaction, however, is the response of some super-spiritual people who believe that all negative emotions are wrong or, at least, unworthy of the truly "Spirit-filled" Christian. If someone shows an emotion like sadness, these people may opine that, "a true Christian ought always to be joyous." To those reading this chapter, did anyone ever tell you that you were less than "spiritual: because you felt or, worse, *displayed* a "negative" emotion like sadness?

Dr. Dan B. Allender and Dr. Temper Lengman, III, in a marvelous book entitled *The Cry of the Soul*, wrote, "Emotions are the cry of the soul. Emotions are the cry that gives the heart a voice. To understand our deepest passions and convictions, we must learn to listen to this cry of the soul." (Dr. Dan B. Allender and Dr. Tremper Longman III, *The Cry of the Soul*, Nav Press, Colorado Springs, 199, p. 25). If you are now experiencing a "down time" in your life, what does that tell you about what is going on in your heart, your soul, or the rest of your life? What does it say about the state of your relationship to God? The opinions of others about that do not matter as much as what you discover.

There is no doubt that bearing a continual burden of sadness gets wearisome. Emotions connect a person to things that are going on in his or her life.. And sometimes the connection seems to be more than we can stand. We get tired of the up and down times, the times things don't go as we want. We get tired of being threatened or, at least, *feeling* threatened. And we get tired of the gloom that can settle in over us.

There are people who feel that such emotions are "improper". They say, "Just get over it; God is in control." But their remonstrations don't sound so much like counsel as criticism, even rejection. They act as if the emotions themselves are wrong.

Some people believe a real person of faith would approach life and its problems with completely unruffled confidence and self-control. However, if you are the one suffering through sadness, you know there are times that you just don't feel "in control." You try to release the sadness but the sadness won't release you. The last thing you want or need is the descendants of Job's friends offering you their inconsiderate and unkind "help."

Anyone may be the recipient of such unwelcome counsel. But ministers, because their lives and reactions are always on such open display and under such microscopic examination, perhaps come in for more than their share of criticism in this area. It's probably not that people think ministers can be perfect, but that people have in their minds a catalogue of which emotions are appropriate and which are not.

It is wrong to assume that sadness, which may come from many sources, is always an "inappropriate emotion." Yet, many pastors face that reaction. They suffer their sadness in silence. It may lead them to deny their true emotions and cover them with an artificial happiness. That, in time, will lead to even more disturbing feelings within, such as feelings of being a fraud. The effort to fake joy can also take a terrible emotional and physical toll on a person by draining his energy. Remaining mired in silence, unable to speak his true feelings, may cost him his ministry more quickly than will revealing his true self.

Sometimes, the lack of "down emotions" just means a hard heart, not a strong faith. Some people were brought up to cover their true emotions. It is reported that when John F. Kennedy, Jr. was a boy, he once took a nasty fall. As he lay on the ground crying, an aide to his father said, "Kennedy's don't cry." John, Jr. reportedly responded, "This Kennedy does."

Some people believe we should use all sorts of mental or spiritual techniques to change our emotions. Some even turn to the use of alcohol or illegal drugs to block out the feelings. There are certainly appropriate times for taking legitimate medications to restore balance to one's thinking or body chemistry. But dependence on only artificial substances solves nothing. The problems, or the wrong thinking about problems, are still there.

Would the critics of "inappropriate emotions" say the same thing to the writers of the Psalms? The book of Psalms is remarkable for the pouring out of human emotions, many positive, but many negative. God has them recorded in His inerrant Word, I believe, to show that emotions are legitimate. We don't need to just "get over" our emotions, or to be stoic, leaving them unexpressed. Emotions tell us how we are dealing with life and God.

Even more, would these critics say to the Lord Jesus that it was inappropriate for Him to feel sadness? He did. When faced with the abandonment of many of the people who had once gladly followed Him, Jesus said to His disciples, "Will you also go away?" (John 6:67) It is hard to miss the deep sadness in His words, even though we cannot hear the inflection in His voice.

When faced with His impending crucifixion, Jesus went to pray in the Garden of Gethsemane. The gospel according to Matthew records these words,

"Then cometh Jesus with them unto a place called Gethsemane, and saith unto the disciples, sit ye here, while I go and pray yonder. And he took with him Peter and the two sons of Zebedee, and began to be sorrowful and very heavy. Then saith he unto them, My soul is exceeding sorrowful, even unto death: tarry ye here, and watch with me." (Matthew 26:37-38)

Jesus was already feeling the oppression not just of physical pain, but also the anguish of being made sin for us.

This was God in flesh experiencing and expressing sadness. Was He, therefore, unspiritual?

Psalm 13 is a marvelous example of allowing our emotions to tell us how we are dealing with life. It was written by David; probably at the time, he was running from the murderous ragings of King Saul. David's circumstances were dangerous. His heart was in pain. He felt low. Read again these familiar words, and take note of His emotions, which some would call "negative".

"How long wilt thou forget me O Lord? For ever? How long wilt thou hide thy face from me? How long shall I take counsel with my soul, having sorrow in my heart daily? How long shall mine enemy be exalted over me? Consider and hear me, O Lord my God: lighten mine eyes, lest I sleep the sleep of death; lest mine enemy say, I have prevailed against him; and those that trouble me rejoice when I am moved. But I have trusted in thy mercy; my heart shall rejoice in thy salvation. I will sing unto the Lord, because he hath dealt bountifully with me." (Psalm 13:1-6)

What emotions do you find bubbling over from David? If you say, "anger, frustration, or doubt," you would be right. But I find a deep underlying sadness in this man, who was, nonetheless, called "a man after God's own heart." David felt God's promise he would be the next king over Israel had not been fulfilled. It is, therefore, probably not reading between the lines too much to say that he may have felt God had not been totally fair with him, that God could have done more to deliver him. Call that "expectation," which led to feelings of disappointment, which brought on a profound sadness. His thinking and reasoning might have been in error. His faith might have been weak. But were his emotions wrong? They were, after all, how he *truly felt*. Please note some things from David's heart-wrenching cry, about where to go when you feel low. It is critically important that you:

Face Your Emotions

Psalm 13 has been nicknamed by some, "The how long Psalm," because it begins with four "how long" questions, such as "How long will this take? How long will this go on?" I ask those questions every time I make a telephone call and get put "on hold." But this is asking *God*, "How long?"

David thought he had been forgotten by God. He said, "How long will you forget me, forever?" Have you ever grown sad because you felt that God put you in an unimportant ministry, in an unknown place, then forgot you?

To deal with your feelings of sadness, it is important to note how negative emotions can make us exaggerate, "God *never* hears or responds to me." Our head, informed by what we know about God, says, "He hasn't forgotten me." But our heart, awash in sadness, tells us something else.

David thought he had been forsaken by God. "How long will you hide your face from me?" he cried out. In the Bible, one's face is often associated with giving attention. Most of us know, intellectually, God's promise in Hebrews 13:5, "I will never leave you or forsake you." But it is easy, emotionally, to *feel* forsaken. Perhaps, the worst thing about facing sadness is believing we are alone.

Many kinds of circumstances can make us feel as though God has forsaken us—some related to the ministry, some not. A tragedy, a crisis that goes on and on, attacks that never relent, a rebellious child, a lingering illness, a problem in the church that brings its ministry to a screeching halt—the possibilities are endless. Self-pity can set in and make us believe that God has abandoned us. Prayers seem unanswered, we can't sleep, the very thought of food brings feelings of nausea.

Emotions are not very dependable guides to life because they tend to show only our perception of the situation, not necessarily the reality of the situation, and lead us to wrong conclusions. In facing a situation that creates feelings of deep sadness, it is important to remember, you *might* be seeing things incorrectly. Emotions do influence us, however, and it is important to acknowledge, "That *is* how I feel."

David said, "How long must I wrestle with these thoughts and feelings? I have constant sorrow." Nighttime is often the worst. Sadness seems to settle in with its heaviest oppression at night. Even when we start to feel better, something inside may seem to restrain us. A man I know who suffered with this kind of weight told me, "I began to feel better, and even started to sing along with a chorus I heard on the radio. Then it was as if a voice said to me, 'How dare you sing? You feel too bad, and the situation you are in is too bad.' So I quit singing and began to sink back into my sadness."

The translation of verse two is interesting, , "How long shall I take counsel in my soul?" The idea expressed is that David is trying to figure out his situation himself and to solve it himself, and he is only making things worse. The more he ponders his dilemma, the more impossible it seems, and the sadder he grows.

That is a natural response when you feel hurt and feel that God is not helping you. You try to fix things yourself. Your wayward child has not changed despite repeated praying. The situation with your church board that has created gridlock in the church has not changed. So, you try to manipulate these things, and everything grows worse.

Then, David pleads with the Lord, "How long will my enemy triumph over me?" He was tired of being attacked.

Your sadness may come from the same situations David faced or from any number of other circumstances. Believe it or not, that intense sadness you feel may have its source in a *physical problem.* Hormonal or other chemical imbalances within the body can result in feelings of sadness. That is why—if you continually feel down or sad, if those feelings are abnormal for you, or if they do not go away by themselves within a few days—you should get a medical examination.

Presuming there are no physical causes, your sadness may trace back to *unmet expectations.* Any expectations, especially unrealistic expectations, may set you up for disappointment and sadness. Pastors are especially vulnerable to such feelings. Pastors tend to have high expectations of how Christians should live and act, how churches should function, and where a particular church should be going in its mission. When things are going poorly—when a church reaches a point of stalemate or the church fragments because of conflict—disappointment and sadness may fall on the leader.

Some pastors feel threatened by such negative events in the church. Especially those pastors who already struggle in the area of self-image may feel *they* are responsible, which, of course, produces deep sadness. When church members also hold the pastor solely responsible, the sadness is intensified.

Pastors who have experienced such events more than one time are likely to develop emotional struggles that go beyond mere sadness. Not all pastors are driven into the depths by concern for themselves, however. Some, particularly those who have invested many years in one church, may feel a sadness that is generally motivated by a concern for the future of the church and its people. In a sense, that may be suffering with Christ, who, of course, grieved and even wept over the hardness of people's hearts.

Sadness may be the result of *the build-up of anxiety, anger, or fear about stressful circumstances.* A middle-aged pastor discovered one morning that his daughter who was working in another city had moved in with her boyfriend. The afternoon, he had a serious automobile accident. The following day, his best friend had a heart attack and died. Two weeks later, his son was arrested on a charge of participating in a burglary. One month later, his father died. All the while, there was a power struggle going on in his church that resulted in a group of people leaving to form another church. There ensued what he would later describe as "his private hell," a time in which he felt as though he was in a pit engulfed by darkness with no way out.

He tried valiantly to tell himself that people other than ministers experienced such deluges of suffering without falling apart. Why should he be any different? If anything, he thought, as a minister, he should be more "on top of things" than anyone else. In this case, the expectations were of himself. The more he thought he should rise above his feelings, the more disappointed he became in himself and the deeper the personal darkness became. Do you find yourself anywhere in this story?

Such events and our response to them can produce what we often call, "the blues," a fairly mild sense of being down, which generally resolves on its own. However, some people may feel an even more intense sadness which interferes with their work, their rest, and their relationships. Some even experience the kind of numbing sadness we typically call clinical depression. Depression not only interferes with people's lives, it controls them. But again, because many people expect the minster to be *above* such feelings, they are never spoken of, so the minister suffers alone, often to the point that he self-destructs.

Depression and sadness may come because of *perceived failure*. The vast majority of pastors are conscientious about their work. Most want to succeed for the right reasons. They want to reach people in order to build the kingdom of God.

Some, however, have a need for success to fulfill some inner motivation gone awry. Some are perfectionists. Failure of any kind cannot exist in their world. Virtually all pastors are competitive. The talk at Monday morning pastor's conferences proves that. Virtually all of us have been influenced by worldly standards of achievement more than we know. We feel that we have to leave monuments to ourselves. The results always have to be better to prove that we were here and that we were successful.

We remember times we didn't succeed and how embarrassed we were. We don't ever want to feel that way again. So, we cannot fail. Guilt feelings overwhelm us when we do fail. Depression often follows hard on the heels of real or perceived failure.

The real problem often is that the intense push for success has robbed us of intimacy with the Heavenly Father. Ultimately, God desires relationship with us more than success in our work. The realization is liberating when it fully settles on our souls. Relationship with Him ultimately satisfies the heart more than leaving a mark does.

In a wonderfully poignant and even convicting remark, Dr. C. W. Brister wrote, "Depression may *feel* like God's anger for human sin or failure. More likely, it is the mismanagement of one's feeling cut off from God, the loss of approving relationships, that intensifies the pain of depression," (C. W. Brister, *Caring got the Caregivers,* Nashville, TN: Broadman Press, 1985, p. 167).

Whenever you are confronted by emotions such as this, face the truth of what you are feeling. Say, "I am sad. In fact, I am feeling very sad." We do not need deliverance from our emotions. We may need deliverance from the wrong conclusions that led to our sadness. We may need deliverance from the lies our emotions make us believe. But our emotions tell us how we are dealing with life. Only by facing and acknowledging our feelings can we get on to the truth.

Further, when you feel low—

Cry Out to God

The Psalmist cries out, "Look on me." That is an appeal for God's attention and faithfulness. He is even so desperate that he says, "If you don't do something, if you don't show me where all this is headed, if you don't lead me in hope, I will die." I have personally known that depth of sadness; have you?

Our emotions literally can tell us if we are moving toward God or away from Him. For example, a person may be feeling shame over a particular sin. Despite repeatedly asking forgiveness, the feelings of shame continue. That may show that the person has moved away from an intimate relationship with the Lord, in which he could be healed with the balm of forgiveness and acceptance. Instead he feels unworthy of intimacy with Him. The negative emotion, once faced, could be the key to discovering the problem.

Perhaps the "negative emotion" is continual anger at being criticized or mistreated unfairly. The problem might be an unwillingness to allow God, the righteous Judge, to handle the situation. The person holds onto resentment or seeks revenge, and the anger stays.

In the case, of deep sadness over the circumstances of life, the problem may be a failure to consider the depths of God's goodness and the totality of His control, even in times of suffering. For example, David is focusing only on the length and depth of trial. He asks, "How long?" If you focus only on the length and the depth, how bad it is and how long it has lasted, of course, you will feel despondent. Focus instead on the goodness and greatness of God. Tell yourself the truth, instead of lies.

When David cries out, "Look on me and answer, oh Lord my God," he uses two different Hebrew names for God: *Elohim* and *Jehovah*. *Jehovah* stresses God's faithfulness. It is the covenant name for God. *Elohim* is a name which stresses God's abundant power.

David has been tempted to feel, with his emotions, that God's promise that he will become king will never be fulfilled. However, he chooses, with his will, to call out to God with names that reflect his faith, not his feelings. "This is how I feel, Lord! Nevertheless I know…that you are faithful and powerful. All is not lost because of who You are!" This is not merely some sort of "positive confession." This is telling himself the truth instead of the lies with which his feelings would deceive him.

If you are feeling anxiety or fear, it might be because you are asking the wrong question. You might be wondering, "Is life predictable?" The answer is, "No, anything can happen." With that kind of focus, fear is a natural result. Change the question to, "Is God dependable?" The answer is, "Yes, He is faithful and dependable to His people."

When you are feeling overwhelming sadness, you might be asking, "Is life just and fair?" The answer is, "No." Change the question to, "Is God fair?" The answer is, "Yes, He is." So our cry must be directed to God.

In the midst of his sadness, David begins to talk to God about some other positive things. He says, "*I will trust.*" (verse 5) Trust is an exercise of the mind and spirit, not the emotions. The ability to trust is grounded in God's character. We can trust because God's love and goodness are unchanged and unchanging. Emotions change. Circumstances change. God's love does not.

Further, he says, "*I will rejoice.*" (verse 5) Rejoicing sometimes must be a decision of the will. Those who are laboring under the burden of profound sadness may find this completely foreign. But the decision to rejoice is grounded in God's promises. His deliverance may not come on our schedule. It may seem slow. But it will come. The issues that so overwhelm you now *will* pass.

Finally, the musician says, "*I will sing*" (verse 6). Singing can give a lift to our emotions. Once again, we can sing because of our matchless and unchanging Lord! Not every Christian has a voice, but every Christian has a song. And it is a song of hope. So, we have the choice, we can sing or sink.

There is one further very important step to take that the Psalmist took.

Confront Your Uncertain Emotions with the Facts of the Situation

Our emotions are God-given, but they do not always lead us to the truth about our situation. The same situations that produce feelings of sadness may get distorted by those same feelings. Despair colors everything differently. One minister said, "I know I tried to look at everything through **WOES**-colored glasses."

David says, "The Lord has been good to me." Our negative emotions may trick us into forgetting the goodness of God's character, His love, and His blessing in the past. That, in turn, will only increase the tailspin of torment we feel.

By faith, when you are low, remind yourself of God's goodness. No, you don't know when your circumstances will change. But you can base your hope of better things tomorrow on God's goodness in the past. Your sadness and depression may well stem from short-term memory.

The Psalmist's answer to sadness and frustration was to look to God. That is also the foundation for our recovery. But there are other things that may help in dealing with sadness. And be sure that we are talking about dealing with sadness, not becoming resigned to it, or comfortable with it.

This chapter has been an encouragement to face the emotion of sadness. Whatever brought it on may or may not have been a wrong assumption, but it *is* how you feel. This chapter is most assuredly *not*, however, an encouragement to remain under the leaden cloud of sadness. It is not permission to suffer alone on the one hand, feeling abused and misunderstood, just masking your silent pain. It is also not, on the other hand, permission to say to those you serve, "This is who I am. You are stuck with a melancholy minister. Don't try to change me, because I am not interested in changing myself. Get used to it."

It is not unspiritual to fell deep sadness, no matter what some people say. However, it may be unspiritual, at times, not to avail yourself of the resources, both divine and human, to deal with the feelings of sadness that are preventing you from experiencing a life and a ministry of true joy. Here, then, are some other suggestions.

Confront your fears, or they eventually will produce sadness and depression. If conflicts with people, reproducing fear; sometimes, open conversation, especially with a third party present, may help allay those fears. You may understand them and their goals better, and what's more, they may understand you and your goals better. We often fear what we do not understand. It is a virtual certainty that deep fear, if not confronted, will eventually lead to feelings of being threatened and to depression.

Be sure you are not tricking yourself into a depression. One pastor was dealing with a variety of thorny issues in the church, some of which centered on a dissatisfaction among some members with him. However, he made things even worse for himself by inventing a variety of imaginary scenarios. The problems *were* real. There was even a potential threat to his ministry. But he not only believed in the reality of the problems, he convinced himself that all his other beliefs about what would happen, what he thought people were saying, etc., were also true. He sank even lower into paralyzing sadness, which only added to the criticism of him.

His gloom even drove away many of his supporters. One man who had sought to encourage the pastor at every turn, finally grew weary and exasperated, and said, "You are just too heavy a weight." Don't let your imagination run wild. Don't build your whole mood on things that may not even be true.

Find someone who will ask tough questions or say the tough things to you. When you are sinking into sadness, that kind of confrontation is often necessary. Give a trusted person the freedom to say to you, "You just might be imagining things." Sometimes, this confrontation might come through professional help. Don't be afraid to ask.

This next matter is extremely important. *Be sure you are not using your moods to get attention.* That can happen, even without your realizing it. You wear a long face, either faked or genuine, so that people will ask you, "What's wrong?" That gives you the opportunity to tell a sad story so that people will feel sorry for you, or even so that you can manipulate them. It has been done! While we want people to allow us to be a human enough to feel sad, we are not to use that sadness as a means of control.

Often, *a time of physical separation from the circumstance* can restore perspective and lift the spirit of gloom. Is it time for a sabbatical leave or extended vacation? Many churches would be willing to grant such time away if it meant they would get back a minister who is happier, more relaxed, and more at peace. You will know the proper channels to go through to see if that is possible.

How Can the Church Help?

The church itself can help its minister live through the times of sadness he experiences. If you, as a church member, recognize the signs of a build-up of stress, if you see a pronounced change in mood, love him enough to ask about it, instead of gossiping about it. Chances are that your pastor has poured out much of his life for you, and ministry can take a heavy toll on a person, physically and emotionally.

Allow the pastor time to share his personal hurts, fears, uncertainties, and struggles. Encourage him with written notes, verbal praise, with material gifts and adequate time for rest. Allow him to bleed the red blood of humanness, but also to occasionally show the grey moods of humanness. Allow him to be a real person that worries about his health, his children, his retirement, and his church. And never use against him the things he shares.

The church that loves its pastor should never *cause* him to become a casualty. It should also never even *allow* him to become a casualty, if it is in the power of the church to minister to him in return and encourage him when he is burdened with sadness.

Sometimes the Situation Is Real

But sometimes, despite all the conversation, the recovery of perspective, and the adjustment of thinking, you discover the situation you are facing is real. The threats you perceived are real and cost you your ministry. The stalemate in the church continues and things grind to a halt. The sadness, it seems, was justified. Then, more than ever, you need to discover the resources God gives. The question is—will you go to Him, or will you just continue to sink into the pit?

Remember, David begins this Psalm by asking God, "How long?" Most of us focus on how long our situation has gone on and how long God is taking to change it. Maybe God is also asking, "How long?" "How long before you will allow me to encourage you and change you?" The more we focus on how long God is taking, the less we will be able to focus on how good God is.

Blaise Pascal (1623-1662) was one of the greatest thinkers with which God has ever graced the Christian community. He was a scientist, philosopher, and writer. During the time of great stress in his life, when he suffered stinging criticism from colleagues in both the world of science and religion, and the death of his sister, Pascal fell into a profound sadness. Later, he wrote, "I have lived with three great delusions in my life, the delusion that I could shape my own destiny, the delusion that I could create my own happiness, and the delusion that I could create my own security. It was out of suffering that I came to see how foolish I had been. And it was also out of suffering that I was led to know God as my trusted friend." (Quoted in Gerald Mann, *When the Bad Times Are Over for Good,* Brentwood, TN: Wolgemuth and Hyatt, 1992, p. 28)

We are not called just to "get over" our sadness. We also are not called to be immobilized by it. Recognizing the cause may tell us what is right or not right about our life or our walk with God. Resting in the fact that He is our friend may be the key to easing out of the night of sadness back into the daylight of joy.

Chapter Six

The Unspoken Burden of the Ministry: Disappointment

The old pop rock song came blaring from the pastor's car radio, "Why do you build me up, just to let me down…then you turn me around…and worst of all, you never call…when you say you will…but I love you still…." He knew he was in one of his "moods." People around him called it a "blue mood." He preferred calling it a "reflective mood." As he heard the words of the song, he muttered aloud, "That's my life all right. I am always set up to be let down." At that particular moment, he was driving home from a meeting with a family in the church, who had told him that they were going to join another church in the area. He remembered the time their family had been in a crisis, and he, along with many other church members, had loved and supported them. Now, they were acting as though none of that mattered. The feeling of disappointment welled up from deep inside. It even felt like a betrayal.

When he heard the words, "…but I love you still…" he hastily snapped the radio off. He knew the feeling of "let down" of which the song speaks, but he did not see how he could continue to love these people. The hurt he felt at that moment was too great. If he had not invested so much time, energy, and prayer in them, it wouldn't hurt so badly, he thought. And it wasn't even fear over the loss of their tithe. He truly cared about these people.

Virtually everyone reading these words has experienced this kind of disappointment, and worse. Pastors are no exception. But how do pastors handle disappointments? Some become resentful. Some continue on with enthusiasm. Some grow cynical and withdraw emotionally. Some leave the ministry. Surveys of churches that have dismissed a minister reveal that the number one reason is a fundamental lack of relationship skills by the minister. Though I have never seen a survey about the following statement, based on my observation and experience, I suspect that one of the main reasons pastors leave the ministry is the build-up of frustration and disappointment.

The usual definition of disappointment is something like this: "Disappointment is what we feel when the actual experience of something does not match what we expected it to be." Disappointment is painful. It makes us feel isolated. Disappointment can trigger feelings of self-pity. Dr. Ravi Zaccharias, a Christian apologist and evangelist, once said, "The loneliest moment in life is when you have just experienced what you thought would bring you ultimate fulfillment and it let you down" (Veritas Forum, Harvard University, 1996).

Disappointment goes deeper than surface emotion. In my experience, disappointment is a hurt in the heart so deep, that if we are not careful, it may cause us to *lose* heart. Pastors are not only vulnerable to disappointment, they may be among the most susceptible to such feelings. In an earlier chapter, there is a reference to the idealism of most pastors. They expect believers to act differently from those still in the world. Pastors expect the church, gathered believers, to desire to honor God, to obey God, to reach people, to welcome people, and to care for people.

Pastors invest a lot of trust in people. They depend on church members to keep their promises, to be faithful to and supportive of the church. Pastors care what happens to people. Most pastors desire the best for people. When the sheep don't follow through, or when they demonstrate less than serious spiritual interest, the shepherd feels more than a simple let down; he feels hurt. A pastor may wonder if he just cares too much. But is that the problem?

There are three major areas in which people may feel disappointment—circumstances, people, and (Dare I say it?) God.

Disappointment with Circumstances

In order to assure you that all God's servants experience this, think of the life of missionary Paul. You could almost open a Bible to the book of *Acts* and, from chapter thirteen on, simply close your eyes, put your finger down, and have it land on words describing a disappointing circumstance in his life. However, the one that possibly brought him the most disappointment is referenced in Romans 15:23-26, 28-29.

> "But now having no more place in these parts, and having a great desire these many years to come unto you; whensover I take my journey into Spain, I will come to you: for I trust to see you in my journey, and to be brought on my way thitherward by you, if first I be somewhat filled with your company. For now I go unto Jerusalem to minister to the saints. For it hath pleased them of Macedonia and Achaia to make a certain contribution for the poor saints which are at Jerusalem…when therefore I have performed this, and have sealed to them this fruit, I will come by you into Spain."

Paul deeply wanted to travel to Spain, but this was not simply a desire to see the world as a tourist. Because Paul was a man with a map of the world on his soul, his passion was to preach the Gospel in Spain. Writing these words to friends in Rome, the apostle made it clear that Spain was on his itinerary and his "To Do List."

But it likely did not happen. When Paul reached Rome, it was as a prisoner. He spent years as a prisoner there, sometimes in a dungeon, sometimes under a sort of house arrest. At one point, he was apparently released and may have traveled some. There is no firm evidence, however, that he ever made it to Spain to preach. When he was beheaded in Rome, the dream ended along with his life. The circumstance didn't work out.

Any minister could think of numerous circumstances in which there was a letdown. A well-planned event simply flopped. A long anticipated or anniversary trip was cut short by a death back on the "church field." A much needed salary raise was promised, then not included in the proposed new budget. We pin a lot of hopes on certain circumstances and, so, frequently have those hopes dashed. Our spirits wilt like the pressed rose from the ninth grade prom.

Disappointment with People

Once again looking at the life of Paul, we can almost hear him speak in the minor key of disappointment in 2 Timothy 4. Paul, in writing his protégé, Pastor Timothy, cites several examples in which trusted friends, who should and could have been like supporting steel in his life, collapsed instead. Most notable are these verses:

> "Do thy diligence to come shortly unto me. For Demas hath forsaken me, having loved this present world, and is departed unto Thessalonica, Crescens to Galatia, Titus unto Dalmatia. At my first answer no man stood with me, but all men forsook me: I pray God that it may not be laid to their charge." (2 Timothy 4:9-10, 16)

At the hour he needed them, his friends did not come through. The letdown of people hurts worse than the letdown of circumstances, precisely because they *are people*. Somehow, we know deep down that we really cannot depend on circumstances, nor can we control circumstances. However we know that people have free will. They make choices. So, we expect them to act out of the motivation of love, or loyalty, or friendship. When they do not, the hurt is great, because it feels remarkably like rejection.

Disappointment with God

Sometimes, we feel we must not say the words, "I am disappointed with God," or if we do say them, we feel we must not speak above a whisper. The Psalmist apparently had little reluctance to voice such complaints.

"Awake, why sleepest Thou, O Lord? Arise, cast us not off forever. Wherefore hidest Thou Thy face, and forgettest our affliction and our oppression? For our soul is bowed down to the dust: our belly cleaveth unto the earth. Arise for our help, and redeem us for thy mercies sake." (Psalm 44:23-26)

How many saints, suffering in silence or toiling in obscurity, have dared to think, or even cry out, "Lord, You forgot me! You could have helped, but You didn't." They are saying, "I am disappointed with God."

You may not have verbalized it, but it is likely that you have thought it. We have been taught that God is in control of everything. It is in His power to fix anything. When He doesn't, we wonder why. Of course, bad things *can* happen to anyone, but pastors may, at times, feel that since they have given their devotion and service to God, they *should not* experience such hurt.

None of these disappointments—with circumstances, people, or God—is peculiar to ministers. However, we may feel that because we are supposedly spiritually advanced, if bad things do happen to us, we should not feel disappointment. If we *feel* disappointment, we should not admit it to anyone, lest we lose prestige or credibility in the eyes of people. After all, what would they think of their pastor if they knew he was angry at God? In fact, to speak of being disappointed with God could cost us our jobs! So, we bear those feelings in silence. We may even think silence is a mark of great faith.

It probably is not necessary to give specific examples, but I will. See if you have ever experienced anything like the following true events, related by people I know. If you have experienced these things, try to remember how you felt. Did it feel then, or does it still feel now, like the burning of disappointment?

A pastor works for several months with the search committee of a church in another state as he considers an offer to become their new pastor. After asking many questions, he is satisfied that the church is a theological match with him, and that the congregation is stable and open to change. Once he agrees to the church's "call," he works with the committee to prepare for a new ministry and on the details of his move.

Upon arriving and digging into the new work, however, he begins to discover dynamics about the church that are not at all like what he was led to believe. The church is actually divided and controlled by a few wealthy families. He is given all the responsibilities of the ministry with none of the authority of leadership. The search committee does not back him. In fact, they seem to have disappeared. It becomes obvious that he has left a church where he was loved and secure, for one where he is treated as a stranger. His future in the ministry is even in question. Disappointment, mixed with insecurity, create a minister unsure of his role, and hesitant to try and lead.

A minister with worship and music responsibilities asks the senior pastor if they can meet regularly to discuss the church's worship services. He would like to develop a closer personal relationship with the pastor. He shares with the pastor some personal struggles that are creating some hurt and tension in his life. First, the pastor says that he is "too busy" to establish a regular meeting time. One week later, the music minister learns that the pastor shared some of his private information with others in the church. Disappointment plus feelings of betrayal create an impossible working situation for the staff member.

During the first ten years of a twenty-year-ministry, a pastor sees twelve young men and women indicate that they feel a call into the ministry or the missionary field. He feels that this is one of the crowning achievements of his service to God and to the church. During the next ten years, however, only three of those young people actually follow through. Disappointment settles in over the pastor's heart. He cannot discern whether his feelings of being let down are personal or are a concern for the overall work of God's Kingdom.

A church staff works together with a team of laypersons on a major event. A sizeable sum of budgeted money is spent. The aim is to discover viable prospects for the church. The planners anticipate an attendance of more than three hundred people; but on the day of the event, only twenty-five members actually attend. None of the members brings any guests with them.

An associate pastor makes a commitment to personally disciple a new convert—a man who came out of a raw past of addiction and manipulation. For four months, the pastor meets weekly with the man to study the Bible. Several times, he answers a telephone call at 2:00 A.M. and goes out to support the man when he is fighting temptation. The minister truly believes that the new "brother" is sincere about his profession of faith and gives money from his own pocket to support him while he is "looking hard for a job."

One day, while at the office, the pastor receives a report that the man has resumed his destructive behavior. Even worse, he is spreading the story that "those people at that church never really cared" about him. He is, therefore, looking somewhere else for a church home.

Have you read your story anywhere here? Not all pastors could have written the previous chapter on sadness, because not all experience sadness profoundly. Not all will experience the problem of being compared to others. But *every* minister could write this chapter because every minister has known disappointment.

We ministers are particularly vulnerable to disappointment. It is probably inevitable that we will tie our feelings of success or failure to what happens in people's lives or to what happens in our churches. That kind of pressure is sometimes self-imposed, or imposed by a denomination. Disappointment goes deeper than an emotional feeling of being "let down." It may also contain elements of feeling rejected, bewildered, and even betrayed.

Disappointments would be easier to handle if they all came at one time. However, sometimes they seem to pile up and overlap. As a friend once said, "I was *set* up to be *let* down so many times that I finally *broke* down."

Disappointment may feel even more poignant and profound if something in our past has made us especially vulnerable. If our parents continually broke their promises to us, if we looked for the "perfect" spouse or church, then things fell apart, we may be conditioned to believe that we are destined to be hurt.

Disappointments come when we feel our genuine efforts are not appreciated. Another friend who was in youth ministry told me of a confrontation with a church member. The man claimed to be coming as a friend, and to be speaking in love. He suggested that, for his own good, the pastor should make more close friends, even "buddies" in the church, especially with the parents of the youth.

The pastor responded that, in his day, he was advised that was not a good idea, but that he would try. The man went on to say he also needed to be more gregarious. Again, the pastor responded appreciatively, and said he would try.

What he did *not* say was that for two years he had been seeking to do both those things. He thought that he had been doing a good job. His wife had seen the change. Apparently, however, this man had not seen the change. Disappointment filled the pastor's heart.

The Cause of Disappointment

The key problem leading to disappointment is expectations. We expect to be appreciated and compensated. We expect to be told the truth. We expect people to be consistent and to follow through on their commitments. We expect our efforts at leadership to be supported.

In the 1970's, I attended a popular seminar being held at many places around the country. The teacher attributed all disappointments to expectations. Using Philippians 2:5-8 as a text, he said that we should give up our right to expect anything at any time. Reflect on those verses for a moment.

"Let this mind be in you which was also in Christ Jesus: who, being in the form of God, thought it not robbery to be equal with God: But made himself of no reputation,and took upon him the form of a servant, and was made in the likeness of men: and being found in fashion as a man, he humbled himself, and became obedient unto death, even the death of the cross. "

Jesus voluntarily gave up his right to the glories and praises of heaven to assume the burdens and limitations of being a man. The teacher said that if we gave up all rights and expectations, God would give us back the things we need. However, we would then regard those things as privileges, and be grateful for whatever we received.

By that line of thought, a minister should give up all rights in regard to the church, or the response of people. By giving up the right to expect *anyone* to show up for a regular or planned event, the minister would then be both grateful for and blessed by anyone who showed up. He would then be nicer to be around, and would affirm those who did come.

That principle could be applied to any number of situations that confront the minister virtually every day. And, basically, it is a valid principle. It is certainly better, using the previous example of church attendance, to be grateful for those who do come than to angrily lash out at them because of those who do not come.

But are *all* expectations wrong? Apparently not, from the perspective of God's Word. For example, the New Testament holds up high standards of conduct for believers, now that we have come out of the world. We are called "the children of light" as compared to "the darkness" (1 Thessalonians 5:4-6). Believers are to hold each other to those standards, so much so that Paul calls us to "warn the unruly" (1 Thessalonians 5:14). That is holding an expectation of Christ-like behavior.

Certain churches hold high expectations as a prerequisite for membership. Written requirements about giving, attendance, service, and other involvement are shared with, and must be signed by, prospective members. Thom Ranier, in his book, *High Expectations: The Remarkable Secret for Keeping People in Your Church* (Broadman and Holman, Nashville, 1999) makes the point that, contrary to what most people might think, those churches are experiencing remarkable growth. The very fact that there are some expectations attaches value to the institution or the cause.

Having said that, a high degree of internalized expectation of people may lead to a high level of frustration and disappointment. That is especially true if the minister also ties his self-worth to the performance and response of people.

Expectations may be the chief cause of disappointment. But one kind of expectation may help in dealing with disappointment. That is, *expect* there to be *some* disappointments in your life. *All* Christians, even the mature leader-types, *will* act like humans being at times. There will always be circumstances for which we will not understand the purpose.

There are many possible responses to the disappointments of life. There are several which are common, but also completely inadequate. You can choose to **fake it**. You can pretend it doesn't matter, when it does. People who suspect that you hurt may admire what they assume is a great attitude or strong faith. But you will not be honest with yourself.

Another alternative is to **be hurt**. You can take every disappointment personally. If people do not support an event you planned and promoted, you can take it as a rejection of yourself. This is especially easy when you have given of yourself sacrificially. But to take every disappointment personally only increases your pain.

You can **lash out**. More than one fiery sermon has been the result of some pastor using the "sacred desk" as a "bully pulpit" to express his own anger. This is rarely helpful, and usually dangerous.

Or you can **give up**. You can simply say, "I poured my dreams into that proposal, only to have it rejected. I spent hours planning that event to have so few come. I just won't plan any more." Repeated disappointment can lead to cynicism and disillusionment. One pastor wrote in his church newsletter, "Let not hope prevail, lest disappointment follow." Many have followed that gloomy counsel. Instead of dreaming, they give up; they don't try anything, for fear of being hurt.

A final option is to **move on**. Some pastors assume that if one church won't respond to them, another will, then another and still another. In some cases, a move might be necessary. On some cases, that is done too hastily.

If those are inadequate responses, how can you respond to disappointment in a way that is healthy for both yourself and those around you? First, you must **acknowledge** your disappointment. Jan Stoop and her husband, Dr, David Stoop, make an interesting point in their book, *Saying Goodbye to Disappointments* (Thomas Nelson, Nashville, 1993). They say that with every disappointment, there is a grieving process. We must express the hurt appropriately. Often that is just to ourselves, or it may be to a trusted group of friends.

You might say, "I was disappointed, and even hurt when the church voted not to buy that property adjacent to the church. There will be some opportunities that we will miss because of that and it makes me sad." Having said that, you can move through the normal stages of grieving, right through to acceptance, and even learning from it.

Another possibility is to **think clearly**. The reason your idea was rejected *might* be personal, but it might not. If you assume that it was personal when it was not, you may develop a defensive or even hostile attitude toward those who oppose you

A few people may let you down because they don't like your ideas or agenda. Most do it inadvertently. If they don't support an event you put on the church schedule, it may simply be because they are more concerned about their own schedule or agenda or dreams than they are about yours. What you consider to be an exciting opportunity that can't be missed, they see as just another thing they have to add to their day.

Of course, that might reflect their own spiritual immaturity or apathy. But if you think clearly, you realize that it is better than convincing yourself that they are rejecting you.

If you assume personal responsibility for the failures in the people's lives, then disappointment will feel very much like personal rejection when it may not be.

Frankly, in dealing with disappointment, it is imperative that you **be patient**. Most pastors want their people to grow to be their best selves in Christ. Could your disappointment with people be because you believe you know what is best for them when they haven't gotten to that point yet? Could your disappointment be because you have established goals for them, as measured by their attendance and involvement, which they have not yet set for themselves? Could it be, therefore, that part of the answer to your disappointment is greater patience with people in their spiritual progress?

Please, if you are thinking about giving up, **try again.** You cannot avoid all disappointments in ministry. The only way to do that would be to remain totally passive. It is dreams that lead to expectations, and expectations that lead to disappointments. But to eliminate disappointments by ceasing to dream is surely not the answer.

We are made to hope and dream. Somewhere, I clipped a statement from a pastor who said, "I was tired of disappointments, so I decided to give up all dreams and expectations, so I would never be disappointed again. The odd thing about it is, deep in my heart, I kept hoping that even that resolution would one day change."

Don't give up the dreams! That would be a dull life. Go back and try again.

Then, **press on**. If a pastor moved on whenever he was hurt or disappointed, he would be a gypsy, never establishing real roots, *or a real trust!* That kind of ministry is, in a sense, a set-up for disappointment, a sort of vicious cycle. People don't know whether to respond to you because they don't know if they trust you. They don't know if they trust you because you haven't been there long enough. Give them a chance to learn to trust you. Endure some disappointments now, for the possibility of reaping the fruit of trust later.

Look at the contrast between these responses to disappointment.

Fake it.	Acknowledge it.
Be hurt.	Think clearly.
Lash out.	Be patient.
Give up.	Try again.
Move on.	Press on.

Which way do you think is the healthy and spiritually mature way of responding? The answer is obvious.

Another incident from the life of the Apostle Paul indicates what surely must have been a tremendously disappointing circumstance and a healthy response.

> "Now when they had gone throughout Phrygia and the region of Galatia, and were forbidden of the Holy Ghost to preach the word in Asia, after they were come to Mysia, they assayed to go into Bithynia: but the Spirit suffered them not. And they passing by Mysia came down to Troas. And a vision appeared to Paul in the night; there stood a man of Macedonia, and prayed him, saying, Come over into Macedonia and help us. And after he had seen the vision, immediately we endeavored to go into Macedonia, assuredly gathering that the Lord had called us for to preach the Gospel unto them." (Acts 16:6-10)

This passage describes Paul's second missionary journey, this time with a new teammate named Silas. Paul had wanted to preach the Gospel in Bithynia. He was somehow prevented by the Holy Spirit. That must have been a disappointing moment. Certainly, he thought about the unsaved people who could have heard of Jesus for the first time. Paul undoubtedly had his own strategy for evangelizing that part of the world. But the Holy Spirit had other plans.

Rather than resist the Spirit, Paul and his company turned toward Troas. That night, Paul had a vision, the description of which has been the source of many effective missionary sermons. "A man of Macedonia" asked for Paul's help. Once again, instead of resisting the Spirit, Paul made ready to leave for Macedonia, now northern Greece, believing it to be God's will. So began what was to be one of the most successful church planting and Gospel preaching times of Paul's life.

This was no smaller matter. By working through what was surely a major disappointment to Paul, God moved the Gospel from

Asia to Europe. Paul gave his most significant service through the leftovers of a disappointment.

In a famous sermon on this text, Dr. Harry Emerson Fosdick said,

> Wanting Bithynia and getting Troas, how familiar an experience that is! But to take Troas, the second-best, the broken plan, the leftover of a disappointed expectation, and make of it the greatest opportunity we ever had, how much less familiar that is! Yet, as one reads the story of human life, one sees that powerful living has always involved such a victory as Paul won in Troas over his own soul and his situation…. Whatever else was shaken when he got to Troas, his conviction still was there that God had a purpose for his life, that if God had led him to Troas there must be something in Troas worth discovering, that God's purposes included Troas just as much as Bithynia, that God never leads any man into any place where all the doors are shut (*Handling Life's Second Bests,* Harry Emerson Fosdick, as quoted in *20 Centuries of Great Preaching,* edited by Clyde E. Fant, Jr, and William M. Pinson, Jr. Word Books, Waco, 1971, p.57, 58).

In order for us to handle our disappointments and experience God's best for us, we must keep the attitude that He is always working out a purpose. Everyone will have disappointments. No one gets all their first choices. It is learning to accept second choices, and to make the most of them, that marks us as mature and makes us useable by God.

The Responsibility on the Church's Shoulders

It would be simple to say, "Don't disappoint your pastor. Attend every service. Always tithe. Be as excited as he is about

105

every ministry of the church. Keep growing yourself. Keep the commitment you make." And those do sound like very good things to do!

But sometimes, the reason people don't respond is that they don't feel their pastor *should* have expectations of them. Perhaps you are one of those. You feel that his expectations of you are too rigid, too confining, too demanding. After all, the church may be his life, but you have a life *away* from church. So you may feel his standards are unfair, even legalistic.

Think about it awhile, though. Do you really want a minister who does *not* expect the best things of you? Earlier, we said that expectations attach value to something. In your pastor's mind, the expectations he has for you are the things that will lift you higher, make you happier, even more successful. His expectations of you often reflect the fact that he thinks you are capable, and gifted, and able to make a real difference.

The reason for encouraging you about church attendance or personal holiness is not necessarily just because he wants to see *his* numbers and statistics grow. It may well be because he truly believes that a larger group of you meeting together for encouragement and growth can produce a larger spiritual army making a larger difference for God where you live. Believing the best about his motives may be the best possible first step to getting pastor and people moving together.

Realize also that your pastor may live with expectations that are putting tremendous pressure on him. Many of those expectations are also unreasonable and unfair. If he does not visit everyone who has the sniffles, in the minds of some, he is not a good pastor. If he is not "filling pews" on Sunday, or increasing the number of baptisms or confirmations each year, he is not being successful.

It is easy, because of the pressure, for the pastor to let his sense of self-worth, success, and even job security become tied to visible results. So, he puts the pressure on you. Could it be that regular doses of affirmation by individuals and by the church could help raise his sense of self-worth, success, and security? Here are some suggestions:

- Tell him frequently that he is doing a good job, if indeed he is.
- Have the members recognize his birthday and his anniversary at the church.
- Send him and his wife on a trip.
- Volunteer to do hospital visitation for him one afternoon, so that he and his wife can go on a picnic. Buy the picnic food for him!
- Slip occasional "foldable gifts" to him when no one is looking; then, put no demands on him in return.
- Brag on him in the presence of others.
- Offer to create a "dream team" to listen to his ideas for the church and to implement as many as possible.
- Give him a raise without begrudging it.
- Win someone to the Lord and bring him or her to church as a candidate for membership.

This will really make him soar!

Disappointments *will* always be a fact in the ministry. But where pastor and people are both committed to reasonable *and biblical* expectations of each other, and are willing to assume those expectations for themselves, both will be happier. One thing is certain: Happy pastors usually tend to produce happier churches, and happy churches produce happier pastors.

Chapter Seven

The Unspoken Crisis of the Ministry: Family Failure

Pastor Wilton Herman settled into his brown leather easy chair for a final look at his sermon. He had long made it a practice to go to bed early on Saturday night and he was ready. The house was quiet because his teenage son was out with friends. His thoughts were briefly disturbed by the doorbell. He heard his wife's quiet steps as she tiptoed to the door, then he heard a muffled conversation. She stepped into his study with fear in her eyes. The towel over her arm couldn't cover her shaking hand. "Someone needs to see you…a policeman," she stammered.

The moment the pastor saw the uniformed officer, he knew instinctively it was about his son. Thirty years in the ministry, and two years of watching his son's lifestyle had given him knowledge of what could happen. The thought flashed quickly through his mind, "You knew something bad could happen; the signs were there. You're not the only family in this situation. Other families have gone through this and survived." But at that moment, he felt singled out in all the universe for a distinct pain. His face flushed and a sense of dread overwhelmed him.

"Pastor," the officer said almost apologetically, "Your son is in the county jail. He was arrested two hours ago and charged with possession of drugs. He will appear before a judge in the morning for bail to be set. I wanted to be the one to tell you." The stunned pastor barely mumbled, "Thank you," and latched the door as the officer left.

In his thoughts, he immediately pictured his son, likely already in an orange prison jumpsuit and in a holding cell with other offenders. "Was he sober? Did he know what was happening?" But as much as he tried to focus solely on his son, and the fear he must be feeling, Pastor Herman's thoughts kept drifting to himself. "What does this do to me and my ministry?" Should I try to preach in the morning or go get my son? How *can* I preach with him behind bars? Will I ever be able to preach again? Who do I confide in to help me know what to do next?"

There is no pain in a minister's life that equals that caused by perceived failure in his family. His family life is the area in which he most wants to succeed. It is the area in which he feels the most influential. He thinks, "I am at home more than I am at church" (which may or may not be true). "I know them better than I know the church family" (he may be fooling himself). "I can, or should be able to control them" (which is almost never the case). He may feel able to control issues in his family since he can't control much of anything at church. So when things go wrong at home, he feels all the more powerless, and feelings of powerlessness can feel very much like failure.

There is no difference in the hurts a minister's family may experience and those of any other family.

- A son fathers a child out of wedlock
- A daughter admits to being homosexual
- A child is arrested
- A daughter refuses to adopt or practice the faith of her father and mother

It may simply be that a minister and his wife seek professional counsel because of struggles in their relationship. Even that can feel like failure, and, sadly, it is sometimes received with unforgiveness and a lack of sympathy by individuals within the church family.

Family problems bring hurt to any family, but there is a particular stigma when a minister's family is in trouble. There is, at one and the same time, a terror of anyone finding out and deep longing to tell someone who will help to share and bear the pain. There is an unsettling feeling that this experience could cost him his position, yet there is also the knowledge that it could give him an even greater ministry by creating a new heart of understanding in him. Focusing on the problem will distract him from his work, yet there is a temptation to run to his work to keep from focusing on the problem. There is a deep feeling of being unworthy for the ministry, yet the conviction that somehow this crisis has not negated his sense of "call." There is the sense that he has been singled out by God for suffering, yet an awareness that he is part of a great company of sufferers, the human race.

Obviously, the circumstances that occur the most frequently to cause "trouble in the parsonage" are rebellious children and marital stress.

Rebellious Children

In most ways, parents in the ministry are like all other parents. They provide for their children as best they can. They want their children to grow up with feelings of security and they want them to be honest, successful, and stable. But for parents in the ministry, a crisis with their children not only affects the children, it can affect the parents' possibility for remaining in the ministry. Knowingly, or unknowingly, therefore, parents may put higher expectation, pressure, and attempted control on their children.

The pastor-father may say, "You can't do certain things because it would affect my ministry." Or he may expect his children to virtually "live at church" because he thinks they have to be role models for all the other children, which increases his status as a role model for all other parents.

Even if their minister father does not apply that pressure, his children may feel it from others. They can feel they are under a microscope, critically examined by everyone from all angles. They may feel pressured to be a perfect example. That can lead to rebellion. Rebellious children often make a pastor feel that he is a failure, and some in the church may have that same opinion of him.

Marital Stress

Ministry can be hazardous to marriage when the pastor's life is not properly balanced. The drains on his time and emotions may make him neglectful of his wife's needs. She may become resentful of the church and retaliate by being less involved with the church and with her husband. She may pressure him to spend more time with her and the children. No doubt there have been many pastors wives who have divorced their husbands because of this issue. Michael Hodgin tells the story of the pastor of a small church who, toward the end of the calendar year, announced to the congregation that his goal had been to visit every family's home before the year ended. He apologized because he knew he would not be able to fulfill that goal. He then asked any family member who desired such a visit before the year ended to raise a hand. Only one hand went up, that of the pastor's wife! (Michael Hodgin, *1001 Humorous Illustrations for Public Speaking*, Grand Rapids, MI : Zondervan Publishing House, 1994, p. 182).

Assuming he is not deliberately attending more to the church than to his home because of personal need issues or to avoid his family responsibilities, such pressure can create feelings of guilt and stress within him. He feels called to be a pastor, yet knows he is also called to be a husband and father. He may feel it is more "holy" to be a committed pastor than a committed family man, but knows deep down that is a wrong assumption.

With the extreme demands on a pastor always increasing, the war within rages, and the war at home intensifies. It can be extremely difficult to know how to alter one's priorities and schedule. So, the relationships at home worsen, and will likely become obvious to people who know him and his family best. Even if the problems do not become known within the congregation, the pastor knows them. Work is not fulfilling because he is not fulfilled at home, so he indeed feels his life is in chaos, which it well may be. Being both a shepherd and a husband distracts and drains a man, even in the best situations. What is needed is a recommitment to both callings. There must be a recommitment to being a compassionate and faithful pastor, but within the context that he will put his family commitments first. That probably will not mean more hours at home than on the job. However, it certainly will mean that he will not neglect his family for the sake of his job, and he will occasionally say, "No" to ministry opportunities when they interfere with a family commitment. Perhaps, not surprisingly, a man who determines to be a better husband and father usually becomes a better pastor, one the church family appreciates and values even more. That is undoubtedly because of the effect this reprioritization of values will have on his moods and his sense of well being.

Biblical Examples

Admittedly, the modern circumstance of being both a paid staff member of a church and a husband and father does not have an exact biblical parallel. However, there are two examples of men who labored as servants of God amidst trying circumstances at home. One truly did see the results of neglecting his family in the rebellion of his children, which must have burdened him terribly. The other was in a troubled marriage, apparently by the direction of God, a circumstance which seems strange to us, but which resulted in a powerful example of the steadfast love of God.

A Neglectful Priest

1 Samuel 2:12 simply makes this disturbing statement,

"Now the sons of Eli were the sons of Belial; they knew not the Lord."

Eli was a priest and judge over Israel for forty years. He was also the priest charged with the upbringing and training of the future prophet, Samuel, who had been brought to the Temple by his mother Hannah, while he was just a young boy. There is no suggestion that Eli was corrupt or neglectful in his priestly duties. Indeed, at times he showed wisdom (1 Samuel 2:12-17, 29). However, he seems to have neglected the raising of his own sons, Hophni and Phineas, who also served as priests. They were guilty of using their priestly authority to steal some of the sacrificial animals brought to the Temple by worshippers and of keeping the best meat for themselves to eat (1 Samuel 2:12-17, 29). Even more horrifying was his sons' lack of sexual self-control with the women who assisted with worship in the Temple.

1 Samuel 2:22 declares,

"Now Eli was very old, and heard all that his sons did unto all Israel: and how they lay with the women that assembled at the door of the tabernacle of the congregation."

Clearly, Eli knew about the practices of his sons. Either because he felt powerless to change the circumstance or perhaps because he was afraid of his sons, he merely rebuked them verbally. His words seem rather weak and impotent.

"And he said unto them, Why do ye such things? For I hear of your evil dealings by all this people. Nay, my sons; for it is no good report that I hear ye make to the Lord's people to transgress. If one man sin against another, the judge shall judge him: but if a man sin against the Lord, who shall entreat for him?" (1 Samuel 2:23-25a)

The Scripture plainly says that Eli's sons paid him no attention.

"...nothwithstanding they hearkened not unto the voice of their father." (1 Samuel 2:25)

Perhaps they had little or no respect for him. Perhaps he was "all talk," never having backed up his words with proper discipline. More likely, they were just rebels who had completely hardened their hearts against the Lord. That seems likely because the Bible says they had reached such an advanced stage in their sinfulness that

"...the Lord would slay them." (1 Samuel 2:25c)

God never makes such judgments lightly!

Indeed, the boys did lose their lives in a battle against the Philistines as the judgment of God. (1 Samuel 4:10-11). But there was also another penalty on the house of Eli. God said,

"Behold the days come, that I will cut off thine arm, and the arm of thy father's house, that there shall not be an old man in thine house. And thou shalt see an enemy in my habitation, in all the wealth which God shall give Israel: and there shall not be an old man in thine house for ever. And the man of thine, whom I shall not cut off from mine altar, shall be to consume thine eyes, and to grieve thine heart: and all the increase of thine house shall die in the flower of their age." (1 Samuel 2:31-33)

The lingering effect of Eli's neglect of his family responsibility was powerful. It is difficult to imagine that he did not feel a sense of grief, shame and failure over his family situation as he tried to minister before the Lord. Eli also died tragically, as he received the news of his son's deaths, and the Israelites' defeat. Later, his grandson, the son of Phineas, was named Ichabod, conveying the meaning, "the glory has departed from Israel."

Few pastors would deliberately ignore or neglect their families as Eli may have done. Few would deliberately be inconsistent as Eli may have been. But his experience does serve as a warning about the importance of a pastor seeing his family as his first shepherding responsibility. The consequences of not doing so can be greater than just feelings of pain and failure.

When Things Are Wrong in Marriage

There is a strange command given by God to his prophet Hosea, recorded in the book that bears Hosea's name.

"The word of the Lord that came unto Hosea, the son of Beeri, in the days of Uzziah, Jotham, Ahaz and Hezekiah, kings of Judah, and in the days of Jereboam the son of Joash, king of Israel. The beginning of the word of the Lord by Hosea. And the Lord said to Hosea, Go take unto thee a wife of whoredoms and children of whoredoms, for the land hath committed great whoredom, departing from the Lord. So he went and took Gomer the daughter of Diblaim; which conceived and bare him a son." (Hosea 1:1-3)

This odd command seems very much unlike God, who had previously told his people to marry only those who also loved and served God. But this instruction to knowingly marry a prostitute and to raise the children of her other lovers as his own was to later convey a powerful message. God repeatedly told Hosea to take back his faithless wife and to forgive her, as a picture of God's own steadfast love to his faithless people

With a little imagination, we can put ourselves in Hosea's place. How could he serve God, and speak for God, while wondering where his wife was and who she might be with at that very moment? This distraction must have been powerful! Hosea clearly loved his wife, Gomer, with a true love. Any feelings of failure were not because of a lack of trying to serve her, but because his servant love had not broken her heart and caused her to be faithful to him.

He knew he had been obedient to God. He knew he had given his best to Gomer. Still, he must have wondered about his fitness to continue serving God.

There are some scriptures that refer specifically to a pastor's responsibilities at home. Consider these seriously.

"This is a true saying, if a man desire the office of a bishop, he desireth a good work. A bishop then must be blameless, the husband of one wife, vigilant, sober, of good behavior, given to hospitality, apt to teach; not given to wine, no striker, not guilty of filthy lucre; but patient, not a brawler, not covetous; one that ruleth well his own house, having his children in subjection with all gravity; for if a man know not how to rule his own house, how shall he take care of the church of God? Not a novice, lest, being lifted up with pride he fall into the condemnation of the devil. Moreover, he must have a good report of them which are without, lest he fall into reproach and the snare of the devil." (1 Timothy 3:1-7)

Obviously, the Apostle Paul, by inspiration of the Holy Spirit, says that one who would be a bishop, or pastor, must be known as one who gives attention to his home as well as to the church. He must live and lead with a proper Spirit. It is not legitimate to sacrifice one's home in the name of giving all to the ministry.

Certainly, other scriptures that apply to a man's responsibilities to his family also apply to ministers.

"Husbands, love your wives, even as Christ also loved the church and gave himself for it...let every one of you in particular so love his wife even as himself, and the wife see that she reverence her husband...and ye fathers, provoke not your children to wrath: but bring them up in the nurture and admonition of the Lord." (Ephesians 5:25, 33, 6:4)

Heartache at Home

Let's make this personal. When conflict and disappointment do happen at home, despite all your best efforts, what should you do? Can you keep serving as a pastor, and how?

Don't be surprised by the wide variety of emotions you experience. There will likely be feelings of guilt, shame, anger, fear, self-doubt, mistrust, loneliness, unworthiness to go on serving, helplessness, and abandonment by God. In particular, parents whose children rebel against God or reject the Christian faith may feel anger toward their children for putting them in what they consider to be a precarious position regarding their future in the ministry. They grow angry at the children because of their choices. They are angry at being put in a situation that is out of their control. That anger may blind them to their children's needs. The minister in such a situation may truly begin to think only of himself, his reputation, his income, and his inability to continue in ministry.

Anger itself can make a parent or a spouse unable to function in ministry, and especially unable to help their spouse or child through their own time of crisis. The anger should be dealt with in a redemptive and healthy way, by confession, expression, and release.

Potentially crippling are the feelings of unworthiness for ministry. You may feel unable to preach or counsel with others about their family or emotional issues when surrounded by such mountainous issues within your own family. How can you talk about victory over hurt when you feel defeated by your own hurt? You may even feel that your call is invalidated because you are no longer fit for ministry due to a family crisis. The Scriptures were never intended by God as a tool for self-flagellation, but some ministers use 1 Timothy 3:4-5 in exactly that way.

> "One that ruleth well his own house, having his children in subjection with all gravity, for if a man know not how to rule his own house, how shall he take care of the church of God?"

It is easy to reason that we are at fault for all family failures, so we must be disqualified for God's service. That however, leads to a possible wrong conclusion.

You may feel you are being punished.

Because ministers deal so often with such issues as sin, guilt, accountability, and punishment, you may begin to reason that a family failure is God's punishment for not spending enough time with your family, or not teaching them the Scriptures well enough. However, it is not hard to shift responsibility, to blame the church for taking you away from your family. At the heart of this is another tendency.

You may assume more blame than you would assign.

You may feel you are to blame for all the failures of your children. If you were counseling someone in the same situation, you would encourage them to acknowledge their failures but to remember that children are still responsible for their own choices. Give yourself the same grace you would give others. Let yourself experience the same grace from God that is available to others through Jesus Christ.

You may come to believe that most of the problems in the church are your fault.

We would all agree that the power of the Holy Spirit is essential for the harmony and fruitfulness of the church. We would never want His work to be limited. However, if your family is experiencing any degree of turmoil, you may believe that you and you alone are responsible for grieving and quenching the Holy Spirit. Any presence of problems or lack of power in the church, by that reasoning, must be due to you. It is true the Spirit desires that we be clean vessels, but fortunately, the Holy Spirit is bigger than any one person.

You may become closed off to others, even those who could and would help.

It is easy to focus so completely on your own issues that you are unaware of and unresponsive to others. A pastor who has typically been confessional in his preaching and transparent in his relationships, may find his personal problems to be an area in which he just cannot be open. The church will certainly come to wonder why he has changed.

You may find your family problems to be the ultimate test of your core beliefs.

This could be true in the area of a son who admits to being homosexual. A pastor who has strong convictions about homosexuality may feel so threatened by his son's admission, he changes his stance on that issue. I know of several such cases. This is probably not hypocrisy in the truest sense, but it could show the intensity with which a minister may feel fear about his position and reputation in the midst of a family crisis. He will do anything to get rid of the threat.

When there is trouble in the pastor's family, much of the hurt and fear he feels may be self-inflicted. The feelings of invalidation, loneliness, and unworthiness may not come from the reaction or treatment of others, but from the unrealistic expectations be puts on himself.

Churches Must Respond Fairly

Sometimes, the hurt the minister feels in this area *is* imposed by others. If the words of 1 Timothy 3:4-5 were not meant to be used for whipping ourselves, they were not meant to be unfairly used against others either. Remember those words again,

> "One that ruleth well his own house, having his children in subjection with all gravity, for if a man know not how to rule his own house, how shall he take care of the church of God?"

"Managing (or ruling)" one's house well does not mean controlling people so completely that they neither can nor will step out of line. If you are a reader who believes that it does mean that, remember that the passage also implies that the pastor should "rule" the church well. Do you want or expect that same kind of "control" imposed upon you and the rest of the church?

Certainly, the pastor should give attention to modeling and teaching God's standards to his family. Certainly, he should lead them to mature by instilling love for the Word of God in them. But this is more a warning against an irresponsible person entering the ministry, than it is a requirement that ministers be perfect people with perfect track records and perfect families. If the latter were true, how many candidates would pastor search committees have from which to choose?

Unfortunately, there are scattered churches that so misunderstand those two verses that they have policies in place to remove a minister from his position at the first sign of unruly children (even grown children!), or because of an argument with his spouse that is overheard. It is no wonder some pastors suffer in silence, letting their hurts go unspoken.

Certainly, there *may* be circumstances where a minister is utterly neglectful of his family and his duties to them. But in most cases, that is *not* the issue. Most pastors are faithful, good-hearted people who try diligently to maintain the delicate balance between "professional" and family responsibilities and *try* to tilt their attention in favor of their families. But for many reasons, thing occasionally just go wrong.

If It Happens to You

Beyond the apparent expectation of some churches and Christians that a pastor, to be worthy of his calling, never experience any problems, there is another particular difficulty for ministers dealing with family problems. Again, let us be personal. Who do you talk to? Who pastors the pastor?

Ministers are sometimes encouraged to "make close friends" in the church. Often that is said by people who themselves want the privilege of being the pastor's "best friend." Pastors are encouraged to talk to people in the church about their personal problems. Yet, every pastor likely knows another pastor who has experienced the "boomerang effect" of that kind of openness. They shared their personal struggles, expecting confidentiality, only to have everything repeated and their struggles used against them. So, some find it difficult to trust.

Revealing family problems would not cost a banker or a taxi driver their position, but it might cost the minister. Having said that, *find someone to talk to.* Living in fear that it would cost you your position will keep you from really helping both yourself and your family.

Acknowledge the problems. At least acknowledge them to yourself whether or not the issues become known to others. Denial does not help! Your first response may be to keep it all a big secret to "protect" your family, to not let any word leak out which could bring embarrassment.

But again, easily enmeshed in the desire to protect your family is to desire to protect your own ministry. And many of the ways you try to protect your ministry may be the very things that do *not* protect your family. Secrecy instead of directness is usually destructive. Focusing only on what the church's reaction will be may actually blind you to the real depth of your family's needs.

Keep your perspective. If the problem in your family is a rebellious child, remember this. Even ministers and their wives who try tirelessly and passionately to raise their children "in the nurture and admonition of the Lord" (Ephesians 6:4) have their hearts broken by their children.

Do not necessarily hold yourself responsible! Do not require perfection of yourself! The pastor's children sometimes rebel like other children.

They rebel:

- Because of their own sinful nature
- Because of the pressure of society
- Because of parental pressure
- Because of the pressure of the church

You can actually overprotect them and push then into rebellion. Keep your perspective, the same kind of perspective you would counsel others to keep.

Revisit your priorities. It is always helpful, in the midst of a family problem, to examine how we might be responsible, how we *might* have lost contact with our family, how we *might not* have communicated well enough or been available and approachable enough. When you are with your family are you really there, or thinking about church business or someone's problems? Do you feel guilty about spending time with your family? It will show.

Have you turned your family against the church and its leaders by talking too much about the way they treat you? Or have you talked of the times of affirmation and the blessings received by being God's called servant? Or, is church all you have talked about, period?

Has your parenting style become one of control, legislating behavior, and heaping on more expectations? Are you fun to be with or a grouch and a bore? Do you consistently give your family not only time but the best of yourself? Rebellion within your family may not really be rebellion against God and his standards, but an expression of frustration at not having enough of you.

Many therapists talk about having boundaries or "margins." Make and keep a real day off, a date night with your wife, and regular, fun outings with your children. Turn off the cell phone when you are with them. Make sure your family knows they are the most important people in the world to you and that you love them with all your heart.

A meeting at church that is re-scheduled or missed completely will not leave permanent scars on your family. But continually missing your daughter's softball games when she desperately wants to show you how she had perfected her curve ball will, and can have tragic consequences later.

Get Help. Just because you are a "professional minister" doesn't mean you can handle all problems by yourself. Many denominational leaders now understand the pressures of ministry and the pressures of society on pastor's families, and provide extensive, free, or low cost counseling services for pastors who stay within their own denominational structures. Or, they may provide financial help if a pastor goes outside the denomination for help.

Allow yourself to experience God's grace. Does having a family problem invalidate your call to ministry? Not if we believe in the complete sovereignty of God. God knew the future, and knew you would walk through this circumstance before he put the sense of call on your life. Yet he extended that call just the same.

Now, being morally and vocationally irresponsible is one thing. There are legitimate times to step aside or be set aside. But experiencing, for example, the rebellion of a child when you are honestly giving the best you have to your family and to your ministry is quite another. The call of God on your life is more all-encompassing that one issue. It is, in fact, one thing that should keep you persevering in ministry and seeking to be a more holy, more complete pastor, rather than giving up because of feelings of self-pity or unworthiness. In the long term, the choices of your children, good or bad, do not have to destroy your effectiveness.

You may feel the need to keep your hurts private and wear a mask of professionalism and competence that denies being human or needing the grace of God. Spend more time in prayer, giving the hurt to God and asking for his grace to heal your hurts, or to at least make you able to minister through your hurts.

The way the Lord wants to shape us his servants is by us admitting that we are not able to serve, apart from his supernatural grace and power (see 2 Corinthians 3:5-6). Like the Apostle Paul, we need to know that our weakness just gives God the opportunity to display his power in us all the more (2 Corinthians 12:7-10). When we admit our weakness, we come to appreciate his healing grace and the power of the resurrected Christ more strongly (2 Corinthians 1:8-9, 4:11-18).

Most of all, allow God to assure you that His grace means that your life and your future ministry are potential wells of deep satisfaction, blessings, and joy. The lives you can still see transformed through your work will be ample testimony to your worth as a pastor.

Some dos and don'ts. Do not compare your family situation with that of others. The family of "Rev. Big Shot" may seem perfect compared to yours, but how do you know what heartaches they may have gone through to get there? Comparison ultimately causes us to belittle or even deny the plan of God for *our* lives, and the power for getting us there. Remember the words of Paul,

"For we dare not make ourselves of the number, or compare ourselves with some that commend themselves: but they measuring themselves by themselves, and comparing themselves among themselves, are not wise." (2 Corinthians 10:12)

Do not immerse yourself in work to avoid dealing with the problem. Do not close yourself off to others. Do not allow self-pity or depression to rob you of perspective, hope, and joy. Do not make excuses for yourself, about why you can't change the things you really need to change. Do not take all the blame upon yourself.

Do allow Jesus Christ to fill your heart with grace, strength, and courage. Do allow the church to minister to you. You may find that it will be a validation of your importance and your ministry to them. They may return what you have given to them. It could be one of the most affirming times of your ministry.

One pastor, whose life was touched by the pain of a daughter becoming pregnant at age seventeen, wrote to me the following words, "There is more understanding within churches about this now, because hardly anybody is untouched by similar things in their own lives. God may turn it all for good. After I revealed openly my situation to my church, people began coming out of the woodwork to say they had experienced the same thing. 'Pastor,' they said, 'If this had not happened to you, I am not sure I could have come to talk to you about my situation. That's because you and your family seemed to be untouched by trouble, so I got the feeling that you would not understand or empathize. Now I know you do.'"

The embarrassment caused by a wayward child can ultimately result in more family unity and a renewed commitment to your family, to say nothing of greater pastoral service.

"And we know that all things work together for good to them that love God, to them who are the called according to his purpose." (Romans 8:28)

Prepare your foundations for trust and understanding now. If you have previously earned a high level of trust with your church family, it will make a difference in the reaction of the church should you experience a family crisis.

Teach the church the principle of "returned ministry." We are to especially minister grace and comfort to those who have shared grace and comfort with us.

Be upright and holy in all areas of your life. That will make it obvious that a family crisis is likely not the result of irresponsible living on your part. On the other hand, if a family crisis is just one of many negative issues in your life, they will likely, and perhaps justifiably, be less sympathetic.

If the news of your family struggles becomes known, be open and honest. Above all, do not be deceptive.

Humility is essential. Any arrogance will alienate the congregation.

Learn from parenting how to pastor and vice versa. Did you ever stop to think how alike these two responsibilities are? Being a parent requires one to give direction, discipline, and lots of encouragement. An effective pastor does the same. For their efforts, parents receive back tremendous joy, fulfillment, and pride, as do pastors. Parents find that part of their lives to be wonderfully satisfying. Pastors experience the same thing.

In my reading, I came across the following words from H. B. London and Neil B. Wiseman in their book, *They Call Me Pastor*. Allow them to comfort and encourage you.

"...I know some are grief stricken, because your grown children are not serving the Lord...so you suffer anguish when you see them ignore the faith values you taught them. You pray that they will not throw away the priceless treasures of their heritage.

And so you lie awake going over what you might have done differently. You cry out in prayer during the night hours. "Other parents have made mistakes, too," you argue with God. "Sometimes I didn't know what to do. I did my best. I loved them." But your conscience haunts you. You didn't spend enough time with them. You didn't go to that basketball game you promised to attend. You neglected to read the Bible and pray with them as much as you should have.

Take courage. There is hope. I want to remind every pastor and spouse that God is not through with your children. No matter how old they are, they are still *your* children. And you can still do some parenting. That quiet inner strength that only a stalwart Christian communicates has far more impact on them than you imagine. Rest in the knowledge that God

is at work in their memories because of what they learned from you. Believe it and feed your faith on that fact."
(H.B. Landon and Neil B. Wiseman, *They Call Me Pastor*, Regal Books, Ventura, California, p. 167-170)

Churches that Help to Heal

It is not the responsibility of the church to correct all the pastor's family problems. However, it is the church's responsibility to help create an environment in which the pastor can be free to serve and lead in his home in a way that till help *him* create a healthy home. Remember that ministry puts a person in a unique and often seemingly impossible position. The shepherd is also one of the sheep. He needs tending from the rest of the body of Christ in the same way he seeks to give it. The church can help pastors build healthy homes in several ways.

Give him freedom. Reduce the level of expectations of his children. Expect of them what you would expect of your own children to be normal kids. Seven and eight year olds do not know what it means to be role models for all the other children. Don't require that of them.

Reduce the expectation level of his wife. You didn't get two for the price of one when he came to be a pastor. She doesn't automatically have to be the women's mission society leader, sing in the choir, teach Sunday School and do a host of other jobs. Allow her to serve only in the areas in which she feels called and gifted. Allow her the time to be an attentive wife and mother, first of all.

Help your pastor to develop his marriage by giving him the time and resources to do so. Encourage members to give him some extra money occasionally for a nice dinner with his wife or the night away from home and responsibilities. A pastor serves the church more happily and effectively when things are going well at home.

Give him privacy. Let him know he does not have to always "be on duty" for every minor emergency. If yours is not a multi-staff church where responsibilities can be shared, form a group of trained lay persons who can be "on call" for circumstances that arise during the evenings, or on Saturdays to give the pastor time to be a husband and a father.

If the pastor lives in a church-owned home, let it be his home for the time that he lives there, in the sense that he has privacy. In one church that owned a parsonage, members regularly dropped by for "walk through" visits, to see how their pastor and his wife were taking care of the house. They also routinely left their children with the pastor's wife for babysitting without announcing their arrival. The rationale was that she should be willing to do that in return for getting to live in the house "rent free."

Pastors appreciate privacy perhaps more than anyone else. Their whole lives are already in a fishbowl, open to people's scrutiny and criticism. They will never be able to build healthy homes without privacy.

Give him encouragement. If it is obvious that he is hurting in some area of his family life, be there for him with a healing touch, with prayer, with loving, encouraging words and deeds, and with true Koinonia-fellowship. Return the ministry he had given you in a non-condemning and unconditional way. Give him the gift of being secure in your love. Most churches are proud to be known as places of fellowship and encouragement for other wounded and hurting people. Why should that not be extended to the church's own pastor? Realize that you will get back a wiser and more understanding shepherd.

Our pastor who had walked through the dark valley seeing a teenaged child rebel, told of the pain, loneliness, and vulnerability he and his wife experienced in those days. He also told of how several godly elders ministered to him faithfully. They regularly encouraged him by saying. "Pastor, the Lord is not through with your daughter yet. He is big enough to handle this. We believe you have sought to be faithful in training and teaching her. Claim the promise of Proverbs 22:6,

> "Train up a child in the way he should go and when he is old he will not depart from it."

"They were to me," he related, "God's light, giving me direction in my darkness." It is my prayer that all fellow believers would do that for each other, including for their pastors.

Conclusion

These pages have been focused on hurts experienced by people in vocational ministry. There are certainly other hurts than those described here. For the most part, they are not hurts unique to the ministry. Most people are experiencing in their own lives the problems described here. What make a pastor's situation somewhat different is that he often feels there is no one with whom he can share his struggles.

That may be the truth, or it might be simply that the pastor has not identified someone who would listen, protect his confidentiality, and help him bear the load. Candidly, some pastors have trouble admitting that they even need someone to talk to, someone other than the Lord to bear their burdens. In the minds of many, there is still a stigma attached to seeking professional help. They may think that it is a sign of little faith in God to find a counselor, and certainly they may feel there is something of a risk in confiding in a church member, the risk that the hurts they share may not be kept private. There is even the feeling that admitting to hurt diminishes their authority and standing as a minister.

Hurt and suffering often go along with the responsibilities of preaching the Word and helping to bear the burdens of others. The Apostle Paul, in his ministry, had known *the pain of comparison*. Apparently, his preaching had been compared to that of an eloquent preacher named Apollos (1 Corinthians 1:11-13, 3:3-6). The church Paul founded in Corinth was even divided over the issue of whether they would follow Apollos or Paul. Paul had to make the decision to be himself and to preach the message of the cross in his own way.

"And I, brethren, when I came to you, came not with excellency of speech or of wisdom, declaring unto you the testimony of God. For I determined not to know anything among you, save Jesus Christ and him crucified. And I was with you in weakness, and in fear, and in much trembling. And my speech and my preaching was not with enticing words of man's wisdom, but in demonstration of the Spirit and power: That your faith should not stand in the wisdom of men, but in the power of God." (1 Corinthians 2:1-5)

He had known the pain of loneliness.

"For Demas hath forsaken me, having loved this present world, and is departed unto Thessalonica; Crescens to Galatia, Titus unto Dalmatia.(2 Timothy 4:10)

There had been the extreme hurt of betrayal and abandonment.

"At my first answer no man stood with me, but all men forsook me: I pray God that it may not be laid to their charge.(2 Timothy 4:16)

Other servants of God had experienced *severe persecution.* This was the experience of Jeremiah. Because of his powerful and clear preaching, Jeremiah encountered resistance from a man named Pashur, who was the son of a powerful priest of the time. The Bible say that,

"(He) smote Jeremiah the prophet, and put him in the stocks that were in the high gate of Benjamin, which was by the house of the Lord." (Jeremiah 20:2)

In what must have been a terrifying experience, the prophet Daniel was persecuted.

"Then the king commanded, and they brought Daniel, and cast him into the den of lions. Now the king spake and said unto Daniel, Thy God whom thou servest continually, he will deliver thee." (Daniel 6:16)

So, *why* do people become ministers? Why enter a profession today that:

- In some cases, pays barely enough to support a family
- Is less respected in society than many other professions (and even that level of respect is declining)
- Makes unrealistic demands on a person
- Demands holding and declaring beliefs that are contrary to the basic beliefs of society in general?

There is no reason, except that Almighty God calls them! Being "called" to the ministry is a term popularly used but rarely explained. Some people speak of "surrendering to the ministry" and mean the same thing. Others say, "I didn't have to 'surrender' because I never fought it." But what is a "call"?

No one can completely explain to another person what a "call" is. It has to be experienced in different ways. If there is a common denominator, it is that a call to ministry is a persuasive inner prompting or inner learning. In essence, it is an inward sense of "must."

The Apostle Paul, in shackles and giving his testimony before King Agrippa, related his experience of calling in this way.

"At midday, o king, I saw in the way a light from heaven, above the brightness of the sun, shining round about me and them which journeyed with me. And when we were all fallen to the earth, I heard a voice speaking unto to me, and saying in the Hebrew tongue, Saul, Saul, why persecutest thou me? It is hard for thee to kick against the pricks. And I said, Who art thou, Lord? And he said, I am Jesus whom thou persecutest. But rise, and stand upon thy feet: for I have appeared unto thee for this purpose, to make thee a minister and a witness both of these things which thou hast seen, and of the things in the which I will appear unto thee: delivering thee from the people, and from the Gentiles, unto whom I now send thee." (Acts 26:13-17)

Later, Paul wrote,

"For though I preach the gospel, I have nothing to glory of: for necessity is laid upon me; yea woe is unto me if I preach not the gospel." (1 Corinthians 9:16)

Jeremiah described it in this way,

"Then I said, I will not make mention of him, nor speak any more in his name. But his word was in mine heart as a burning fire shut up in my bones, and I was weary with forbearing, and I could not stay." (Jeremiah 20:9)

Charles Spurgeon saw the presence of a "holy discontent" as the clear sign of a calling to ministry. He often encouraged his students not to enter the ministry if they felt they could be satisfied doing anything else.

All these servants of God experienced the sense of a "divine must."

Sometimes, the sense of call is only a quiet prompting from within. Sometimes, it rages within. Sometimes, it reassures us. And sometimes, it is the only thing that holds us to our task when, in the face of opposition and hurt, we want to quit. But always, there is the sense of holy unrest unless we are in a pastoral vocation. Answering "the call" does not mean that other vocations are unimportant but for the one called, nothing else is as important.

One reason people speak of surrendering to the call as though there must, of necessity, be a clash between their will and the will of God, is that some people believe God would not call someone to anything that brought great pleasure. Even among those already in the ministry, there is sometimes the feeling, "How could God have led me to do this? I like it too much. It brings too much fulfillment." The assumption is that the will of God always involves such suffering, deprivation, burden, and sacrifice that the human spirit would always shrink from it. Where did we get such a distorted idea of our wonderful God?

Not only does such an attitude deny the goodness of God, it also denies his wisdom. To be sure, there are heartaches and hurts that accompany ministry. Certainly, there are times we *do* what we do not *want* to do because inwardly we know we must. But "surrendering to the call" is really more about God creating within us a *desire* and a *delight* to do what we sense we *must* do.

This sense of "must" should not be viewed as compulsion. Certainly, there have been people who felt they must enter the ministry for reasons that were unhealthy:

- the expectations of parents or grandparents
- trying to atone for earlier sin and rebellion against God

- the result of making a "deal" with God in a time of crisis
- escape from another unpleasant career
- the feeling that this is the only way to please or appease God

The real "must," however, is an intense and willing desire to obey God, to walk in His way and to serve Him. Somewhere, I once heard it said that "The sense of the call is where our joy and our burden meet. The sense of call is where our obedience and our gifts meet." We follow because we or others sense gifts of God for ministry in our lives. Of course, not every person who follows the call of God believes they are gifted. In fact, like Timothy in the New Testament, they feel ungifted for some areas of ministry. But they respond to the "must" within, trusting that God will enable them.

The inner sense of "must," in its purest sense, is, or at least becomes, a "want to." That was certainly my own experience.

While in Junior High and High School, people often asked me if I thought I would follow in the footsteps of my pastor father. My standard reply was, "Not the way I see it now." I remember saying those exact word *many* times! At the time, I thought that was an unqualified, "No." Now I realize, I was leaving myself an "out."

During that time, I pondered a number of possible career paths, particularly commercial art. But nothing truly answered the sense of "must" stirring within me. In short, there was nothing I truly *wanted* to do.

During my freshman year in college, I attended a revival service in my home church and had the opportunity to spend time with my father and the evangelist. I took a deep breath and said, "Dad, I think God may be calling me into the ministry." There was a long silence, "Son, I have known that for a long time. I said nothing because I did not want to be the one who most influences you. That is up to the good Lord."

The moment I spoke, the direction of the desire of my life changed. When I uttered the words (for the first time, I might add),

"God might be calling me," I went from not knowing what I wanted to do, to knowing there was nothing *else* I wanted to do, or *could* do. It was the sense of a "divine must." That certainly has, at times, been the one thing that has held me to my course when walking through valleys of hurt and discouragement. Every minister who has been in the work for a while has experienced the same thing.

The Lord continues to call people into his service in the same way. At times, I have hesitated to talk about the burdens and pain of ministry (especially to young people who had already felt God's call) for fear it would drive people away, or make them less willing to listen to Him. That shows my occasional lack of confidence in His sovereignty and the power of the call. He keeps touching people and they keep responding, in spite of the known challenges.

One thing I must make clear: Pastors are not inherently noble because they patiently endure hurts and persist in their calling. They are just being like their Lord, who endured for greater hurts to fulfill His calling. Long before the descent of God the Son to a womb, a cradle, and a cross, the prophet Isaiah predicted Jesus' endurance in this way,

"He was oppressed, and he was afflicted, yet he opened not his mouth: he is brought as a lamb to the slaughter, and as a sheep before her shearers is dumb, so he openeth not his mouth." (Isaiah 53:7)

The writer of Hebrews, encouraging people to be faithful while under pressure, wrote,

"Wherefore seeing we also are compassed about with so great a cloud of witnesses, let us lay aside every weight, and the sin which doth so easily beset us, and let us run with patience the race that is set before us, looking unto Jesus the author and finisher of our faith; who for the joy that was set before him endured the cross, despising the shame, and is set down at the right hand of the throne of God. For consider him that endured such contradiction of sinners against himself, lest ye be wearied and faint in your minds. Ye have not yet resisted unto blood, striving against sin." (Hebrews 12:1-4)

Paul said to Pastor Timothy,

"Thoutherefore, my son, be strong in the grace that is in Christ Jesus. And the things that thou hast heard of me among many witnesses, the same commit thou to faithful men, who shall be able to teach others also. Thou therefore, endure hardness, as a good soldier of Jesus Christ. No man that warreth entangleth himself with the affairs of this life, that he may please him who hath chosen him to be a soldier." (2 Timothy 2:1-4)

It is Christ who enables us. He makes us adequate for the journey and the task. It is for His sake we serve. It is by His pleasure we serve. And it is through His power we serve. Through the hurts and disappointments, we go on, for the sake of the call! And, in the midst of the struggles, we find the most intense fulfillment and joy ever experienced by a human being!

"The call" creates no exemption from suffering, it may, in fact, increase the suffering. All the hurts cannot be taken out of the ministry. They "go with the territory." They come about because of the "offense of the cross" (Galatians 5:11). They come about because of people's basic sinful nature and pride. They come about because of the clash between tradition and truth. But we can persist in faithfulness by the mighty presence of our living Lord, in whose steps we are following.

"For this is thankworthy, if a man for conscience toward God endure grief, suffering wrongfully. For what glory is it, if, when ye be buffeted for your faults, ye shall take it patiently? But if, when ye do well and suffer for it, ye take it patiently, this is acceptable with God. For even hereunto were ye called: because Christ also suffered for us, leaving us an example, that ye should follow in his steps." (1 Peter 2:19-21)

We often hear that we are to follow in Jesus' steps, follow His example. It is perhaps significant that the only place the New Testament specifically tells us to follow "in His steps" is in the area of suffering. There are hurts that simply accompany ministry. They will always come. It is my hope they will not remain "silent hurts." Churches need to seek to create an environment where pastors are recognized as normal human beings with needs. Mutual ministry is a hallmark of the body of Christ. Pastors need to receive ministry just as they give ministry. There are people who will understand. There are people who will not be threatening, abusive or manipulative with what they know. They will comfort and support their minister. Most of all, of course, the Lord understands.

It is my hope that some church members reading these words will determine that to give the freedom of transparency to their pastor will ultimately make him more effective. It is my hope that they will sense a burden to care for him as he has cared for them.

Perhaps a hurting silent pastor, reading these words, will unburden his heart and find rest, relief and healing. My favorite words of the Old Testament are these,

Thy shoes shall be iron and brass; and as thy days, so shall thy strength be. There is none like unto the God of Jeshurun, who rideth upon the heaven in thy help, and in His excellency on the sky. The eternal God is thy refuge, and underneath are the everlasting arms... Deuteronomy 33:25-27a (KJV)

In your hurt, may you find the healing of Jesus, your ultimate Pastor.

9 780881 441673